Damon Hill

M000309607

Other books by the same author

FERRARI
The battle for revival

WILLIAMS
Triumph out of Tragedy

DAMON HILL
From Zero to Hero

THE QUEST FOR SPEED
Modern Racing Car Design and Technology

DRIVING FORCES
Fifty Men Who Have Shaped Motor Racing

WILLIAMS
The Business of Grand Prix Racing

FIFTY FAMOUS MOTOR RACES

DEREK BELL
My Racing Life

FERRARI
The Grand Prix Cars

BRABHAM
The Grand Prix Cars

MARCH
The Grand Prix Cars

JACKIE STEWART'S PRINCIPLES
OF PERFORMANCE DRIVING

As part of our ongoing market research, we are always pleased to receive comments about our books, suggestions for new titles, or requests for catalogues. Please write to: The Editorial Director, Patrick Stephens Limited, Sparkford, Nr Yeovil, Somerset BA22 7JJ.

Damon Hill

ON TOP OF THE WORLD

Alan Henry

Patrick Stephens Limited

© Alan Henry, 1996

All rights reserved. No part of this publication may be reproduced, stored in a retrieval system or transmitted, in any form or by any means, electronic, mechanical, photocopying, recording or otherwise, without prior permission in writing from Patrick Stephens Limited.

First published in November 1996
Reprinted in December 1996
Reprinted in January 1997

British Library Cataloguing-in-Publication Data:
A catalogue record for this book is available from the British Library

ISBN: 1 85260 566 9

Library of Congress catalog card no. 96-77283

Patrick Stephens Limited is an imprint of Haynes Publishing, Sparkford, Nr Yeovil, Somerset BA22 7JJ.

Designed and typeset by G&M, Raunds, Northamptonshire.
Printed in Italy by G. Canale & C. S.p.A. - Borgaro Torinese (Turin)

Contents

Acknowledgements

I must offer my thanks to Peter Foubister, publisher of *Autosport*, and Michael Harvey, editor of *Autocar* for whom I have been Grand Prix editor during the period in which this book has been written, for permission to quote from their respective publications. I am also grateful to *Motoring News* for permission to quote interview material involving Damon Hill.

I am indebted to Johnny Herbert, Martin Donnelly, Mark Blundell, Eddie Jordan, Patrick Head, Frank Williams, Adrian Newey, Dickie Stanford, Ann Bradshaw, Jane Gorard, Paul Radisich, Nigel Roebuck, Maurice Hamilton, Rothmans UK, *Motorcycle News*, Brands Hatch Circuits and David Tremayne for various assistance and advice during the time I have been gathering information and data for this book.

In connection with the photographic content, my thanks are due to Steven Tee and Kathy Agar of LAT Photographic, Darren Heath, ICN, David Phipps, Eoin Young, Eric Bryce and the Jim Clark Room at Duns, Berwickshire, and Peter Wheale.

At Haynes Publishing Darryl Reach, Alison Roelich and Flora Myer encouraged and cajoled as usual.

Finally, a word of thanks to my son Nick for organising the photographs into some semblance of reasonable order, double checking the proofs and keeping an eagle eye open for any of his father's more obvious errors. Any such are mine and nobody else's.

Alan Henry
Tillingham
Essex
August 1996

Straight from the grid

They crowded into the pit to wait for his arrival. Mechanics, engineers and his wife Georgie. Nervous, agitated, excited. In reality, of course, Damon Hill was home and dry already. But he was still out there, pounding relentlessly round at the front of the field. The Englishman was determined to finish this glorious day with a win. And he did so, with style and panache. It was the culmination of more than a decade of personal dedication, hard slog and commitment. And – for the millions of fans watching on television at home, as well as the hooting, flag-waving, ecstatic crowds at the circuit – this was proof that in an extremely competitive, mega dollar sport, nice men can triumph.

In the pit lane the tension was electric. Old hands, seasoned in the ways of Grand Prix racing, could feel tears welling up in their hard-bitten eyes as they appreciated the historical significance of what they were witnessing. Then, almost abruptly, it was all over. The dark blue Williams-Renault Formula 1 car, carrying race number five on its nose and flanks, burst into view round the final right-hander at the Suzuka International Speedway. A blue-liveried arm emerged from the cockpit and began punching the air. From the pit wall Georgie held aloft a signalling board. It read DAMON, WORLD CHAMPION 1996.

Her 36-year-old husband had just won the 1996 Japanese Grand Prix to become the eighth British driver in history to grasp the World Championship crown. He would have been the new title holder, in fact, whether he had finished or not, because he had needed just one point, and the only threat evaporated when his team-mate Jacques Villeneuve spun off after losing a wheel. But he did it the way he had hoped to, the racer's way.

In doing so, Damon Hill also became the second member of the Hill family to achieve this remarkable distinction, following in the footsteps of his late father Graham, who took the title in 1962 and 1968. As

Damon Hill makes a brilliant start at the 1996 Japanese Grand Prix and leads all the way
(ICN UK Bureau).

with both Graham's titles, Damon kept his fans sweating right up to the last race of the season. Unlike his father Damon absolutely dominated that final round.

In the elation surrounding his success, Damon Hill could reflect that he had rounded off the season as he had started. With a win. Three of his predictions had also come true. After winning the first race in Melbourne, he had confidently observed that every driver who won the opening race of the season for the past six years had gone on to take the title: 'It's a tradition I intend to continue!' Later, when it became clear that he would be leaving Williams at the end of the year, he vowed 'the championship leaves with me'.

The third prediction was poignant. All along Damon had acknowledged his team-mate's calibre: 'I never took the view that this was going to be a walkover. I knew it was going to be close, and I knew I had to make as much of an advantage as possible before Jacques got up to speed and into the swing of things.

'He was a match for me by the end of the season, but I had the added pressure of finishing races and making sure I won the championship. He was coming from behind all the time and could take a lot more risks'.

For the past four races Hill's form had become progressively erratic as Villeneuve stepped up the tension with a late challenge. Yet the Englishman had now reclaimed the decisive form which had given him such a confident edge in the opening races of the season, when he had won four of the first five races.

At Suzuka, although Villeneuve qualified on pole position, 0.4sec ahead of Hill, the Canadian driver made a poor start, and Hill surged away in the lead, beating off an aggressive attack by Gerhard Berger, and was never to be headed, even during his two routine refuelling stops, throughout the 52-lap race.

When Villeneuve spun off Hill knew his championship points total could not be beaten. But he pressed on, determined to end his tenure with Formula 1's premier team on a high note. Discarded by Williams so late in the season that the other top drives were already contracted, he was moving to the TWR Arrows Yamaha team for 1997 in an effort to build a new future from F1's second division.

He even went so far as to acknowledge that this had probably been his last chance to win the World Championship, that the F1 baton might now be passing to a younger generation.

And, it must be said, during 1996 there had been moments when Hill did not seem to drive like a World Champion in waiting. He had made enough mistakes to convince the Williams management two-thirds of the way through the season that Damon's position as title leader was largely because his arch rival Michael Schumacher had temporarily absented himself from the front rank by taking on a new challenge at Ferrari. For 1997 the double World Champion, a close second at Suzuka, believed he would have the car and equipment to win back his title. Villeneuve would be among his main opposition. Hill, felt Williams, wasn't up to the job.

But right now, any such thoughts were forgotten. Jubilant commentators, and the BBC's Murray Walker the most jubilant of them all, were remembering the moments when Hill had harnessed the performance advantage of his Williams-Renault to brilliant effect. He had the best car at his disposal and, as at Suzuka, often performed majestically if he got ahead at the start. This season Hill had given his all and reaped the richly deserved rewards. The bottom line was that he had clinched the title by winning eight of the season's 16 races. And as Schumacher, who had so painfully crushed his 1994 and 1995 title bids, said now: 'Eight wins is something you cannot do with just luck. He deserves this title'.

Damon Hill wandered around the paddock with a broad grin on his face. It was time to savour his success. Everyone was genuine in their delight for this thoroughly decent man who had survived personal tragedy, joined motorsport relatively late, struggled to be taken seriously by the Williams team he joined in 1991 as a test driver, and in only his second full Grand Prix season had to assume the mantle of team leader when Ayrton Senna was killed. Amid a throng of hyper-confident rivals, his self doubts and dignity had won hearts worldwide.

Triple World Champion Jackie Stewart summed it up when he said: 'Damon, more than most World Champions, has had a tough life getting to where he is today. He worked hard for this and has done it in masterful style'. And Hill was typically generous to the team who had sacked him, preferring the unproven Heinz-Harald Frentzen as Villeneuve's team-mate for 1997: 'It was my leaving present to Williams'.

Damon Hill has carved his name into motor racing history. Not only alongside his father Graham, but also with Mike Hawthorn, Jim Clark, John Surtees, Jackie Stewart, James Hunt and Nigel Mansell. Names etched deep into the very fabric of Formula 1. *Damon Hill. World Champion.* Whatever the future might hold, he would always remember this golden moment. The day he earned his place in the Grand Prix sun.

Savouring that glorious moment of triumph — Damon Hill, 1996 World Champion (ICN UK Bureau).

Son of his father

The events of Saturday, 29 November 1975, were largely responsible for shaping Damon Hill's life. As his mother hosted a candlelit supper party for a few friends in the kitchen of Lyndhurst, their elegant 25-room country mansion in the Hertfordshire village of Shenley, just north of London, the 15-year old boy's attention was suddenly drawn to an item on the television news.

Word had come through that a light aircraft, en route from Marseilles to Elstree, had crashed in thick fog on Arkley golf course, a few miles from their home. As his mother would subsequently relate, it took Damon a matter of seconds to guess that this was the twin-engined Piper Aztec flown by his father Graham Hill. He had been carrying five other members of the Embassy Hill Formula 1 team – including the young British rising star Tony Brise – back home from a test session at the Paul Ricard circuit, near Bandol, in southern France.

All those on board were killed. The aircraft had somersaulted to destruction in a ball of flame after its undercarriage apparently hit the trees on the approach to Elstree, Graham's home aerodrome.

Hill senior had flown in and out of the strip on hundreds of occasions over the previous decade since first purchasing the Aztec from winnings yielded by his victory in the 1966 Indy 500 classic. This night, in the filthy weather conditions, rather than waste time diverting to Luton he gambled that his familiarity with the area would see him through. But his luck was out.

The entire country joined the Hill family in mourning for the man whose carefully nurtured public image had made him one of its best-loved sporting celebrities. Tragedies surrounding such famous figures flicker in the public's attention for a few weeks, then dim. Life continues, the world moves on. Yet for Graham's wife and three children – Brigitte, Damon and Samantha – his sudden death at the age of 46 bequeathed them a legacy which was as unpleasant as it was painful.

11

The company which insured the Aztec would not pay out because Graham had overlooked renewing his pilot's licence. The bereaved families of those on board had no alternative but to sue his estate in order to obtain financial compensation. The Hills were effectively cleaned-out. Their grief was compounded by the ignominy of having to move from relative splendour into a modest semi-detached property in St Albans.

In an era when so-called 'sporting stars' are two-a-penny, it may be difficult for the reader to appreciate the status enjoyed by Graham Hill at the zenith of his Formula 1 career more than a generation ago.

Graham Hill was born in a Hampstead nursing home on 15 February 1929. There was precious little about his background or upbringing to suggest he would ever scale any great heights of personal achievement, yet he won the hearts of the British public as a national hero.

Graham Hill, whose sport then was rowing, didn't so much as drive a road car until he was 24. But nine years later the moustachioed Londoner, driving for the British BRM team, had successfully bagged the first of two World Championship titles. At a time when racing drivers were nothing more than sportsmen getting on with the job they loved, Graham was a pioneer when it came to popularising motor racing with the wide world beyond the enthusiast audience.

Here was a man who not only won races, but could converse on television with royalty and ruffian alike, exuding an easy, relaxed, spontaneous charm which instantly captured the imagination. There was nothing dour or stereotyped about Graham Hill, unlike many of today's over-intense sporting technocrats.

He was very much a man's man. The well-timed saucy wink, the mane of dark hair and the well-trimmed moustache all added up to an image of the classic, convivial Englishman sallying forth to do battle on behalf of his country against those marauding hordes of 'Foreign Johnnies'.

Graham had first sampled a racing car in late 1953, paying just £1 for four laps of Brands Hatch at the wheel of an ancient 500cc F3 machine. He found it much to his taste, but the experience led him to ponder on the dilemma facing so many aspiring young talents contemplating a career in this most expensive of pastimes: if he was born to travel first class, it was patently obvious that Graham Hill lacked the price of a ticket.

He managed to surmount this particular hurdle thanks to a well-executed programme of socialising and sheer hard graft. Regularly, he would appear at the bar of the Steering Wheel Club, motor racing's most established watering hole in Brick Street, just off Park Lane in London's West End.

As he later admitted, one glass of beer would last him an evening – most of it evaporating – as he chatted with the motor racing crowd. Eventually he got a job as a mechanic with Colin Chapman's fledgeling

Young fan. Five-year-old Damon Hill (centre) walks with his parents and sisters from the airstrip behind Brands Hatch towards the pits and paddock. Father Graham was off to drive a 2-litre BRM V8 in the 1966 British Grand Prix (Eoin Young).

Lotus team, a key strategic move which would eventually lead to his F1 debut with the team at Monaco in 1958.

He failed to finish, yet in the years that followed he would make the streets of the Principality his personal stamping ground. Throughout the 1960s, by dint of five wins in seven years, he would become hailed with the soubriquet 'Mr Monaco'.

But it was Graham's switch to the BRM team at the start of the 1960 season which really set him off on the road towards serious, sustained success. By the time he led that year's British Grand Prix at Silverstone, only to spin off under pressure from Jack Brabham's winning Cooper in the closing stages, his wife Bette was heavily pregnant with the second of their three children.

On 17 September, Bette gave birth to a boy. Graham wasn't present for the great event as he was away racing at Snetterton, in Norfolk, in company with his famous contemporaries Jo Bonnier and Dan Gurney.

In his autobiography *Life at the Limit* (William Kimber, 1969; reissued by Patrick Stephens Limited, 1993) Graham recalls: 'Bette rang me at 8.30 a.m. on the morning of the race to tell me that I was the father of a son and I was naturally delighted. She says that my first reaction was to ask if that was all she'd woken me up to tell me, but I don't think I was quite as callous as that. The morning after the race, I went straight to the hospital to visit Bette and our new baby boy'.

Interestingly, Damon's birth seems to have passed without mention within the pages of contemporary motor racing magazines. The Pit & Paddock pages of *Autosport* — the bible of British motorsport — were devoted to the social activities at the Anchor Hotel, close to Snetterton in nearby Thetford, where most of the F1 crowd seemed to be staying. It was bursting to the seams, so much so that *Autosport*'s legendary technical editor John Bolster had to kip down in the bar. Bolster, a great friend of Graham Hill, would have hardly regarded it as a privation.

I remember growing up thinking that winning the Monaco GP was Dad's job

The pages also featured photographs of the latest BRM which Graham drove to fifth place, after a spin, in the Lombank Trophy race. The winner was Innes Ireland at the wheel of a works Lotus 18. But no mention of Hill junior.

Not long afterwards, Damon Graham Devereux Hill was duly christened at St Paul's Church, Mill Hill, close to number 12 Parkside, the family's comfortable, unpretentious home in that north London enclave. Soon Graham would depart to compete in the Portuguese Grand Prix for the BRM team.

The tone was already set for Damon's childhood: Graham would be away for much of the time. In the 1960s, before driver retainers had sky-rocketed to the point that no F1 team in its right mind would risk allowing its drivers to compete in other categories, the infrastructure of international motor racing was very different indeed.

Not only did top drivers compete in a full programme of World Championship Grands Prix, but there were many non-title F1 races, touring and sportscar events and, later, the Indianapolis 500 which Graham would win for Lola in 1966 at his first attempt. This meant long absences from home and a potentially complicated relationship between father and son.

For all his gregarious charm, it is hard to avoid the conclusion that Graham Hill was a male chauvinist of the first order. He once confessed that his wife Bette accused him of 'working at everything but our marriage'. Yet there is no doubt that, by and large, it was a happy union. Bette's uncompromising loyalty and devotion shines through in every reference to the man to whom she was married for 20 years. To this day, she styles herself Mrs Graham Hill.

However there was a darkly intolerant side to Graham's nature. Professional colleagues recall that he could be crushingly, dismissively rude if caught at the wrong moment. This was of course never displayed to his public. For the fans, Graham Hill never allowed the mask to slip. Even momentarily.

For the most part, Damon and his sisters retain affectionate memories of their early childhood. Brigitte Hill records the warm and comfortable family atmosphere in the family home at Mill Hill as she grew up. In the 1993 edition of *Life at the Limit* she writes:

'The 'sixties for us – the height of Daddy's career – was a whirl of parties, tons of people at the house, Mummy and Daddy going away and coming back again (our grandmother's cine films consisted almost entirely of us leaving our home at Mill Hill and then returning), interspersed with school, piano lessons, *Doctor Who*, Honey, our retriever, and summer days playing in the street with our friends at Parkside. A normal childhood we thought, and in many ways it was'.

Yet as far as Damon was concerned, those early years of exposure to motor racing left him with a thinly veiled lack of interest in the sport. Even Graham's five victories at Monaco was water off a duck's back. He recalls the afternoon of his father's final victory through the streets of the Principality, during the spring of 1969. It was to prove the last Grand Prix victory of Graham's career.

'The only thing I remember about him in connection with Monaco was when we were staying at a friend's cottage in Kent,' says Damon. 'I was playing in the garden with their son, Nick (the son of former racer Les Leston) and Mum came out and said, "Come and look at Daddy winning the Monaco Grand Prix", and I sort of thought, "Can't I stay out here and play?"'

Damon Hill shows a characteristic childhood boredom with proceedings during the 1967 British Grand Prix at Silverstone. His father Graham is in discussion with his Lotus team-mate Jim Clark (Eric Bryce).

'I must have been eight years old at the time and I remember coming in and watching Dad coming round the old Gasworks hairpin in the red and gold Lotus 49 and sort of finishing the race, and that was it. It didn't impress me at all.'

Much to the frustration of his classmates at school, he hardly ever referred to his father's profession when in their company. Clearly, no man is a hero in the eyes of his family!

'I never came to Monaco with my father,' Damon recalls, 'but I remember growing up thinking that winning the Monaco Grand Prix was his job. That was what he did for a living. We used to go to the Italian Grand Prix quite regularly, combining it with family holidays; but not to Monaco.'

After Graham's death, Bette insisted that Damon took his A-level examinations, after which he enrolled at the South Bank Polytechnic to do a course in business studies. As things turned out, he would not complete the course, and his increasing obsession with motorcycles steered him towards racing on two wheels when, in the early days, he would earn a crust by working as a despatch rider. During this period Damon was also a member of a punk band which laboured under the unlikely title of Sex Hitler and the Hormones.

Two years after Graham's death, Bette wrote her own touching memoirs entitled *The Other Side of the Hill*. Of the teenage Damon, she noted:

'Soon after we'd moved out to St Albans he went out on his moped, then came home. As he had kept his helmet on, I said, "where are you going?"

'"I'm going out," he said as he lifted the vizor and pushed his face forward to kiss me. It took my breath away – his face and everything about him was so like Graham.

'The helmet probably helped to provide a familiar frame to the picture, but the face inside it was so like Graham's, and so were the mannerisms. When I used to ask Graham where he was going, that's just what he said: "I'm going out"'.

From the moment Damon first came into car racing in 1984 it was inevitable that he would be repeatedly compared with his father. This exasperated him to a degree, but he was sufficiently patient, shrewd – and indeed polite – to acknowledge that the media's preoccupation with this particular link was something that was not going to go away.

It was a calculated decision by Damon which would stoke that interest. By selecting his father's distinctive helmet colours – vertical white stripes on a dark blue background, the livery of the London Rowing Club of which Graham had been a member – he virtually guaranteed that he was a hostage to his late father's memory.

Damon responded to this avalanche of interest by picking his words with care. Yet he wasn't prevaricating in any way; here was a man in

Damon and his sisters Brigitte and Samantha play draughts with their father at their country cottage in Kent, February, 1968 (Phipps Photographic).

Emulating Dad. Damon joins Graham for a touch of clay pigeon shooting in 1968 (Phipps Photographic).

his early thirties suddenly being asked for memories of what were obviously rather painful and disrupted teenage years.

The underlying problem was that he had been deprived of the opportunity for personal bonding which is sometimes struck between father and son yet, by the same token, so often fails.

'Rather than dwell on all the detail, I think I can sum it all up by saying that perhaps I'm a bit more experienced (about life) than some of my contemporaries,' he recalled during his first season with Williams in 1993.

'I thought, well, I've been very privileged for the first 15 years of my life, but now I'm going to get on with it like Dad did. He started from scratch and made his own way, now I've had to do the same.'

Damon made a point of not attempting to rationalise the circumstances surrounding his father's death, although he admits that it does seem cruelly ironic that a man who had survived one of the most dangerous eras in international motor racing should retire safely from the sport, only to die in a plane crash five months later.

Interestingly, it was at Silverstone, where in 1994 Damon would win the British Grand Prix and thereby achieve a distinction which his father never managed, that Hill junior's head was almost turned away from racing cars for good.

The occasion was the 1971 International Trophy race, a two-heat non-championship F1 race which Graham won in the distinctive 'lobster claw' Brabham BT34. Yet proud though Damon clearly was of his father, by the time that particular race began his thoughts were firmly planted elsewhere.

Although he had driven a car for the first time at the age of five and would later crash round in a battered old Austin A40, it was to life on two wheels that he now became magnetically attracted.

The 11-year-old's attention was hypnotized by the sight of somebody riding around the Silverstone paddock on a Honda 50cc monkey bike. The owner let him have a go and, as Damon recalls with crystal clarity, he knew that this was absolutely what he wanted more than anything else in the world.

Damon approached his father sheepishly, asking, 'What do you think the chances are?' and he was duly rewarded with one for passing his Eleven-Plus examination. 'I was absolutely stunned,' he recalled.

'I thought it was the best thing that had happened in my life. I've still got it, and from that moment on, I was into bikes. I used to get every bike magazine I could find – about moto-cross, circuit racing . . . anything.

'After I developed that initial interest, Dad got into bikes himself because we had some land on which we could ride. He got a 350cc trials bike from Bultaco, the Spanish maker, which he used to ride round enthusiastically.

'Obviously that was a lot more powerful than my 50cc monkey bike, and I was a bit surprised that he let me have a go. But he just told me to wear my helmet and be careful! After that, I just wasn't interested in the 50cc bike anymore. That was the moment, I think, that I discovered speed and power.'

Damon started bike racing in 1981 on a Kawasaki. He used to ride from St Albans right the way through to south London to help a friend who was working in the building trade, gutting houses in preparation for restoration. All the money he earned went into his motorcycle racing kitty.

'I used to finish putting the bike together at nine o'clock in the evening, borrow my Mum's car, hitch up the trailer and drive up north,' he remembers. 'I'd arrive at the track at about one in the morning, pitch my tent, get up at seven because of the cold, then try to qualify and race. More often than not, I was so knackered that I fell off.'

At the end of 1983, Brands Hatch supremo John Webb organised Damon some outings in an Argo JM16 Formula Ford car for the end-of-season BBC Grandstand series at the Kent circuit. But it proved to be a somewhat mixed experience. As one Formula 3 team owner recalled to *Motoring News*: 'I felt sorry for the kid. He just didn't seem to have a clue what he was doing'.

Damon – who over the years ahead was to suffer more than his

Sombre moment. Fifteen-year-old Damon looks serious as he poses in the cockpit of his father's Hill GH2 F1 challenger on its presentation to the National Motor Museum shortly after Graham's death. Bette and Brigitte Hill stand together with Lord Montagu on their left (National Motor Museum).

share of brickbats from a critical press – broadly concurred with that view however, confessing that the switch to four wheels 'was a total culture shock. All of a sudden, I had to fiddle with the vehicle rather than simply trying to go faster. It was no longer a matter of getting good tyres and checking that the chain wasn't loose – and the cornering was so much faster'.

Perhaps a little disheartened, he went back to bikes for 1984 and scored more than 40 race wins, riding both a Yamaha TZ350 in the Champion of Brands series and an LC350 in the national Pro-Am series, competing against the likes of Neil Mackenzie and the late Kenny Irons.

'He wasn't a slow rider, but, to be frank, he didn't really look destined for great things,' said Rob McDonnell, the Road Race GP reporter for *Motorcycle News*. Yet Damon was still operating on a shoestring, working out of a garage rented by car racer Barrie Williams and using a £50 Transit van.

The young Hill nevertheless seemed pretty satisfied with his achievements. 'There's more a rider can do on a bike,' he insists. 'He's much more a percentage of the package than the bike itself.'

The year 1981 had been a significant time for Damon as it was then that he made the acquaintance of his future wife Susan George, known to her friends as Georgie. 'I first met Damon at a bonfire night party,' she recalls. 'I thought he was a pretty good looking guy. He chatted me up, and impressed me with his seemingly inexhaustible supply of jokes – mostly bad.

'He'd been having some fun with a few other girls I knew, so I had heard a little about him – I knew he was into motorbikes – but I didn't realise at the time that his family had such a racing history.'

Up to then, Georgie admits that she had known precious little about motor racing: 'I'd taken a passing interest in the Grand Prix on Sunday afternoon. I like to listen to James Hunt's commentaries and thought the drivers looked pretty good in their kit!

'At the time we met, Damon was into racing bikes, although as we had met out of season, I had no idea that this meant every weekend when the season was on. I thought he was joking when he told me that was the case. But it was too late. I was smitten by then, and quite happy to squash into a Transit van loaded with bikes and head off up the M1 on a Friday night to places like Cadwell Park.

'He switched from bikes to cars a few years later and into a different world. I didn't have to hold the pit board out! Somebody else had that job. It quickly became a pretty serious occupation and, within another few years of that it was becoming the norm to see his face all over the sports pages on a Monday morning.'

Right *Celebrating Georgie's birthday during the 1995 San Marino GP weekend* (ICN UK Bureau).

Just as his mother had displayed a firm influence during his formative years, so Georgie comes across as a strong personality, albeit in a very different way. And one gets the impression that she is every bit as committed as Damon is to maintaining the family's privacy away from the circuits.

Yet, by the same token, Georgie rejects the somewhat stereotyped notion that being a motor racing wife is somehow a very particular task strewn with unique pitfalls.

'I don't think being a motor racing wife requires any different gifts than being a wife of any successful and high profile person,' she says. 'But that is what marriage is all about, isn't it? Supporting the other half when they need that – it just seems that drivers need it a bit more!

'The constant attention and everybody recognising Damon can be a little difficult sometimes – (perhaps) when we want an evening out together – but, really, the upside outweighs the downside. We're able to live a pretty luxurious life, travel to great places, meet people we wouldn't ordinarily meet and, when the season is over, we are able to have the most fantastic holidays anywhere in the world.

'The lack of time is always the most difficult thing to cope with, but after quite a few years of being a motor racing wife, I think I'd have been bored with a nine-to-fiver. Because, above all else, it is never boring being married to Damon, and absence really does make the heart grow fonder.'

That said, Georgie acknowledges that Damon certainly has committed himself totally to his chosen profession: 'There's no doubt that Damon has a lot of pressure on him. Mainly from himself. He is totally committed to being the best. That means most of the time he's totally immersed in his own world of trying to achieve that goal and, when the season is on, he is usually only thinking of the next race or the next test.

'That can be pretty difficult to live with at times, but it's something I've acclimatised to. As his job in hand has grown, so must the level of his dedication. End of story. I fully support him in that because I want to. Because I love him and want him to achieve what he wants to, because that is what makes him happy.'

Oliver, Damon and Georgie's first-born, arrived on 4 March 1989 and suffers from Downs syndrome. The dignity and courage with which they focused on their son's plight is something which they kept to themselves, but friends confirm that Damon was a tower of strength to his wife in the immediate aftermath of the birth.

The question of putting Oliver into care was never an option. He was a member of their family and that was all anybody needed to know. It was a challenge to be coped with and neither parent shirked the responsibility. Life continued: the Hills knew you simply played the cards which were dealt you.

Two-wheeled love.
Damon leans into
Druids hairpin at
Brands Hatch during
his Yamaha days.

Two wheels or four.
Damon's great
passion was
motorcycles, but
mother Bette
encouraged him to
switch to cars,
believing them safer.

'It was an awful thing for both of us, particularly Georgie,' Damon recalled. 'I think in my twenties I very much wanted to force my own plan on my life. I wanted things to happen my way and tended to battle on in one direction, not allowing anything to affect me.

'But after a while you realise that things are either going to happen or they're not. As long as you can say you've done your best, then you should be satisfied.'

Oliver would later be joined by Joshua, born on 9 January 1991, and then by Tabitha who arrived only a few days after Damon's ignominious retirement from the 1995 British Grand Prix at Silverstone following his ill-starred tangle with Michael Schumacher's Benetton.

I'm adamant that I don't want to do to my children what I went through

By this stage, Damon's financial circumstances had changed dramatically. Mid-way through his second season as a member of the Williams race team, the terraced house in Wandsworth first gave way to the wing of an elegant mansion in Ascot, and finally to a large Edwardian clifftop home with tumbling terraced gardens, facing out over the Irish sea, half an hour's drive south of Dublin.

Late in 1994 Damon had decided that the moment was right to move into tax exile and one obvious benefit offered by Ireland was the fact that Oliver's schooling could be continued in the English language.

'I don't like being away from home,' Damon admits. 'In fact, I hate being away from home. But I love coming to races. It's an interesting point. Perhaps being at home is even more attractive because of its comparative rarity. So perhaps one gets more from being at home because you know you've got to be off somewhere else within a few days.

'One thing I am really adamant about though is that I don't want to do to my children what I went through, the way I was brought up. I was very happy, I was very lucky, and everything like that, but my Dad was never there, never really around.

'But things were different in those days. They raced all the year round. I mean, they went for six weeks in the winter to Australia and New Zealand for the Tasman Series. Every time he got in a car, he was paid. That was the way it worked in those days. Compared with him, I am very lucky. I can earn plenty of money without having to do anything else but drive, so if I can find a balance, then I would be happy to continue racing for a long time.'

In all the conversations the author has enjoyed with Damon Hill over the past five seasons, there has always been a degree of almost formal stiffness when it comes to his comments about his father. He speaks about what they did together, what he achieved, where he raced and where they lived.

24

Yet never has he really given any indication of what he truly felt about the man who left his life so abruptly in the middle of his adolescence. He is too private and dignified to open his heart to an outsider on such a deeply personal matter. Nor, quite frankly, would one expect him to.

It may be that Damon is simply displaying a proper reticence. This would certainly be in line with his behaviour in other matters. He is not an outwardly emotional man who likes to wear his heart on his sleeve. Private thoughts are simply those. Rectitude is the overwhelming quality Damon Hill radiates to outsiders, whether consciously or not.

Even so, it would have been understandable if the aftermath of Graham's death had left Damon ingrained with a sense of indignation and angst. For it was the mismanagement of Graham's affairs which made the family almost destitute and his mother, suddenly a widow in her mid-forties, struggling to bring up her family in such drastically reduced circumstances.

In that connection, I will quote from a letter I received from Dan Gurney, the great American driver who was a team-mate of Graham Hill's at BRM in 1960. Damon went out to stay with him in the immediate aftermath of his father's death, and he recalls the teenager's state of mind:

'My recollection of Damon at that time was one of a young man in deep shock, a young man who was asking such questions as "what is life all about?" and the fact that Graham was no longer with us. I don't know how one learns to cope with it, but that is what Damon was going through.

'I think he spent some time with my oldest son, John, and I think he was looking for essentially something to take his mind off recent events, if at all possible, so he was a young man in a trance to some degree. I'm sure he didn't know what he wanted to do with his life at that time, but he showed a lot of the same natural curiosity and spirit that both his mother and father demonstrated many times in the past.'

On the eve of the 1994 Australian Grand Prix at Adelaide, the race at which Damon would come within a single point of the World Championship, triple World Champion Jackie Stewart offered a warm tribute to his old team-mate's only son:

'I'm really thrilled for Damon, because I think he has had one of the toughest rides that I know of. I've known him since he was a little wee boy, when Graham was my number one driver at BRM.

'When Graham died there were complications about his flying licence, and about the insurance on the plane, and his financial affairs were not left in the best condition. Bette had to move out of a beautiful country estate to a very modest living with three children who were already going to private schools, and then had to be taken

out of those schools because they couldn't afford it.

'Damon left school at 17. He found a very nice girlfriend and they got married. Then their first baby had Downs syndrome, a terrible shock to anyone. He had been a brickie, a motorcycle rider, scratching around to get into Formula Ford because his Dad was Graham Hill.

'Jackie Stewart's son Paul got benefits and little sponsored rides because of his father. Damon struggled to get through, and didn't have his Dad to give him advice like I could to Paul. So he tried to go through F3 successfully, and struggled. Then he tried Formula 3000 and didn't make it because of the finance required. And suddenly a magic wand came along in the form of Frank Williams with a testing contract, and Damon went about that in a very thorough, businesslike, workmanlike and dedicated way.

'He showed himself to the mechanics and the team to be a really serious racing driver. Then Nigel Mansell retired — a fairy tale — and Damon took over the reins and delivered. Immediately delivered. OK, so he had the best car in the world. But you've got to drive it.

'You've got to give the boy an immense amount of credit, achieving what he has done without, clearly, the same amount of experience as a Michael Schumacher and probably many of the other drivers.

'So, when you think of all those things, you've really got to appreciate what the boy has achieved with very little knowledge and experience. I'm not saying for one minute that Damon Hill has deserved any more or any less than he's got.

'I think he's done one hell of a job.'

It is to Bette Hill's credit that her children continued to grow up into such well-rounded adults. In some ways Damon is very much his father's son: the jutting jaw line, the stony gaze reserved for those who cross him, even the almost unconscious, dismissive sniff — so often Graham's trademark — as a prelude to answering a question. And like his father he had no financial advantages but worked his way to the top through hard graft and entirely on his own merits.

Yet in other ways the son is so very different. He is less obviously the life and soul of the party, preferring his own company and that of family and close friends to any wild socialising. The notion of dressing in drag for an impromptu cabaret at a Gentleman's Smoker's evening organised by one of the racing clubs, as his father once did back in the mid-1960s, would probably no more occur to him than flying to the moon.

If Damon Hill ever finds himself wondering 'how the hell did I get here?' let alone 'what made my father tick?' then there are many in the motor racing community who might offer him a sliver of sympathy. As well as a wry grin.

The road to the top

Carving a path into car racing was always going to be a struggle for Damon Hill. While racing motorcycles, he was very clearly his own man, cutting his own career path free from the weight of his father's reputation. Yet that would all change when he moved onto four wheels on a full-time basis.

In 1983, encouraged by his mother Bette, Damon attended the Winfield Racing School at the old Magny-Cours circuit in France, a proven training ground for fresh single-seater talent. 'He was very good on them (bikes), but they were so dangerous they scared me. I thought he would be safer in a car,' she noted.

At Winfield Damon had shown above average aptitude. Towards the end of 1984, after a successful season racing bikes he made the switch to Formula Ford. He won his first Formula Ford race at Brands Hatch and did sufficiently well to pick up a Special Commendation in the end-of-season Grovewood Awards, at that time the British motor racing community's most prestigious barometer of young talent. He then started to gear himself up for a full season of car racing in 1985, securing backing from Ricoh, the office equipment supplies company.

Now it was time to make a serious bid for success in the major-league British Formula Ford series. His challenge was organised by the Manadient Racing Team run by Kevin Barrett. At the wheel of a Van Diemen RF85 he now found himself pitted against the likes of Mark Blundell, Johnny Herbert and Bertrand Gachot, all well regarded and highly focused youngsters whose ambitions would be realised with graduation to Formula 1 in the fullness of time.

Formula Ford was the closest-fought training ground imaginable for aspiring young talent. To gain sustained hard results you needed to be quick, determined and extremely lucky. The margin between success and failure was measured in tenths of a second.

Looking back on the mid-1980s, it is easy to recall the names above because they fought a path through to the sport's higher echelons. By contrast, although Perry McCarthy, Jonathan Bancroft and Paulo Carcasci never became household names, many within the motor racing community believe they could quite easily have done so had the cards of fate fallen in a different pattern.

Damon proved quick and audacious at the wheel of his Formula Ford car. He won six races during the course of that first full season in four-wheeled competition, finishing third in the Esso FF1600 and fifth in the Townsend Thoresen Championships.

There were also a handful of less memorable, if significantly more spectacular moments. Among these was a huge accident at Oulton Park's Knicker Brook corner which resulted in Damon being hospitalised overnight with concussion.

Despite this setback, he bounced back into contention to win his heat and the semi-final at the Brands Hatch Formula Ford Festival, a 38-car annual jamboree at Brands Hatch in which drivers compete both in their own right and as members of three-car national teams. Together with Bancroft and Blundell, Hill's efforts helped Britain to win the team prize.

In the summer of 1985, Hill was invited to test one of Eddie

Cutting his teeth. Damon in action at Silverstone with the Ricoh-backed, Manadient Racing Formula Ford Van Diemen RF85 during his maiden full four-wheeler season in 1985 (LAT).

Damon's Murray Taylor Racing Ralt RT30/86 (No. 17) wheel-to-wheel with Andy Wallace's Reynard as they sprint for Old Hall corner at the start of a 1986 British F3 championship race at Oulton Park (LAT).

Jordan's Formula 3 cars at Donington Park. He turned in some respectable laps, confirming the direction in which he wished to take his career. His best lap was half a second away from that set by the Brazilian driver Mauricio Gugelmin, then one of the British F3 hot shoes who would later graduate to Formula 1 and IndyCars.

Moving up from Formula Ford into Formula 3, the aspiring young racer is faced with the challenge of swapping grooved racing tyres for dry weather slicks. He also has to come to grips with the complexities of chassis 'set-up', those intricate adjustments to rear wings and front flaps which again make the difference between being right on the pace and trailing along in the midfield ruck.

The British F3 championship scene has a long and respected pedigree. Formula 3, as such, had first been conceived in the immediate post-war years with 500cc motorcycle-engined specials providing a much-needed training ground at a time when there was precious little in the way of formal structure to help a young driver advance his career.

In 1964 a young Scot called Jackie Stewart won the British F3 title. The following year he joined Graham Hill in the BRM line-up and set out on a Formula 1 career which yielded him three World Championship titles. The 1983 title fell to possibly the most brilliant racing driver of all time, Ayrton Senna. The young Brazilian had surged to victory driving for the West Surrey Racing team operated by the highly respected Dick Bennetts who would later field the works Ford Mondeos in the 1996 British Touring Car Championship.

In 1986 it was West Surrey Racing that Hill approached in order to lay his own plans for a graduation to Formula 3. Ricoh initially said they would remain as Damon's major sponsor and the idea was that he would partner Canadian rising star Bertrand Fabi in a two-car team. Unfortunately Ricoh then changed their minds and it was back to square one on the sponsorship front.

I'm at my fullest racing and didn't want to reach 60 having done nothing

All was not lost. Damon believed he had another potential backer – Warmastyle – but that company eventually opted to support the national 'Racing for Britain' campaign instead. Damon .was offered a contribution to his budget from RFB. Perhaps rashly, he declined.

Hill explained his plight to David Tremayne, then editor and F3 correspondent of *Motoring News*: 'Ricoh pulled out just before Christmas and, without exaggeration, I didn't leave the phone or office.

'I was there Christmas Day and Boxing Day, putting calls through to the most ridiculous people – some really obscure ones! – just to find something, anything. I was absolutely desperate.

'Commercial deals don't just happen, and after the Warmastyle deal deflated came the problem with the Racing for Britain money. In restrospect, that was the biggest mistake turning down what was offered there.

'The way I saw things, I just had to be racing. I'd been reading one of Niki Lauda's books and I figured that if I was really convinced, I could do it. I would take a gamble and let things sort themselves out. I borrowed a huge sum on the understanding that it will be paid back, and that is exactly what it will be.

'Money still has a fixed value as far as I'm concerned. I did the deal with Dick and everything was set again. We'd bought time to find the money to repay the loan.'

Disastrously, the plans became derailed once again. Bertrand Fabi was killed in a horrifying and very violent testing accident at Goodwood, and Bennetts shelved the entire F3 programme, deciding to switch to F3000 instead for the time being.

'I could have said forget it after Bert's death,' confessed Damon. 'Dick went through the same thing. Everybody questioned the whole reason for racing. The darker side of the sport is thankfully rare, but I'd seen it before.

'I remember Dad coming home one day very, very quiet and saw the news film of Jim Clark's death, but I wasn't too sure what it all meant. I was only eight.

'When Bert was killed, I took the conscious decision that I wasn't going to stop doing that sort of thing. It's not just competing; it's doing something exciting. I'm at my fullest skiing, racing or whatever. And I was more frightened of letting it all slip and reaching 60 and finding that I'd done nothing.

'I was in for a penny and I'd been in for £100,000. I decided I would still go for it but, most crucial of all, I'd do it to the fullest, not half-heartedly.'

With West Surrey Racing out of the British picture for the time being, Hill forged a deal to drive for the Silverstone-based Murray Taylor Racing organisation. Taylor, who hailed from Christchurch, New Zealand – a former journalist who worked with the author on the editorial staff of *Motoring News* from 1972 to 1979 – had built up a reputation as a serious and dependable F3 entrant, which many people felt was at odds with his apparently extrovert, free-wheeling outward image.

F3 insiders rated Taylor's team as possibly bettered only by West Surrey and Jordan in terms of overall operational competence. The Ralt-Toyotas he fielded were certainly enough to offer a decent chance to both Hill and his Kiwi team-mate Paul Radisich.

(Once his single-seater aspirations faded, Radisich would go on to carve himself a formidable reputation as a British Touring Car Championship competitor as a member of Dick Bennetts' works Ford Mondeo team.)

Damon did well enough during his freshman F3 season, finishing the 1986 British Championship in ninth place. His best result of the year was a second place at Snetterton, between man-to-beat Maurizio Sandro-Sala and team-mate Radisich. That season he performed in a workmanlike manner without any fireworks. But many observers were still unconvinced that Damon was made of the Right Stuff as far as a possible future career in Formula 1 was concerned.

Intriguingly, one of those who *did* believe that Damon would make it into F1 was Paul Radisich. 'Yes, I certainly did believe that he would get there,' the BTCC star told the author in 1996.

'It wasn't so much because of his results – you've got to remember that we were both racing Ralt chassis when Reynards were the ones to beat – but because of his temperament. That was ideal and, although he probably didn't realise it at the time, there was an enormous amount of interest in him because he was Graham Hill's son.

'Yes, Damon could certainly drive, and that combined with the way in which he used his name certainly drove him onwards. We had some good times together. Like him, I think I was a fairly serious chap as far as my racing was concerned and we both kept our heads down and got on with it.

'If things went wrong, he was not the sort of guy to shrug it aside; he would be fairly heavy-browed about it all. But I had no doubts that he would get into F1, although I thought that would be as far as it went. I had no idea he would be so successful. The (current) criticism of him because he's got the best car is not valid; you've got to be able to put the package together, which Damon certainly has done.'

For his part, Hill admitted that in F3 he learned a great deal about car control. 'My mechanic, Kevin Corin, showed me how to learn what I should be learning about and Murray was good at helping me keep up my self-confidence.

'You control a car with three things: the power, the brakes and the steering. In F3 there is no power, comparatively anyhow. The brakes are so good that you only use them 50 yards before a corner and, if you have excessive understeer, you are out of control the way I see it.'

For 1987, Damon switched to the Cellnet-Ricoh-backed Intersport

Damon switched to Toyota power for his 1987 British F3 season, but it was a patchy year and his Ralt was dogged by unreliability (LAT).

Racing team. This was run by Glenn Waters, Mario Andretti's mechanic during his 1978 World Championship winning season at Lotus. Damon eventually found himself partnered by Martin Donnelly who made a mid-season transfer to the team.

Donnelly's arrival brought with it confirmation of Hill's early season complaints that the TOM's Toyota engines in the Intersport cars were insufficiently powerful. Changes were made and the duo became strong challengers in the latter part of the season, with Damon winning at Zandvoort and Spa. He finished fifth in the British F3 Championship behind Johnny Herbert, Bertrand Gachot, Donnelly and Thomas Danielsson.

Herbert would later explain that, in truth, Hill had not been a front-running contender that season: 'My main threat came from Bertrand Gachot. Damon wasn't really a threat, but he's stuck to it and driven

well. I've come all the way up through the junior formulae [Hill's experience is more limited] but the fact remains that he's got the job done and has become one of the men to beat.'

In 1988 Hill remained in the Intersport team and won twice, the British Grand Prix supporting race being the undoubted high spot of his season. However, he and Donnelly had some close scrapes, most notably at the Scottish Knockhill circuit where the two men collided at the first corner in the final. Cellnet, the team's major sponsor, summoned them both to its London headquarters the following day and told them they were fired.

Glorious moment. Damon's third consecutive F3 season was highlighted by a terrific win in the 1988 British Grand Prix supporting race. Here he heads Gary Brabham and J. J. Lehto during their three-way scrap for the lead, Hill confidently keeping control to the chequered flag (LAT).

'We had to do a bit of grovelling, I can tell you, over the next couple of weeks to get ourselves reinstated!' admitted Donnelly years later.

In the middle of 1988, Donnelly graduated to Formula 3000 for Eddie Jordan's team. This left Damon — third in the F3 Championship, and with a couple of F3000 races under his belt in the GA Motorsport Lola — facing something of a major dilemma at the start of the following year. A fourth year in Formula 3 was not really on the cards: he needed to progress into Formula 3000, the next rung of the ladder leading towards Formula 1, but the finance was just not available.

In 1989 he trod water with a handful of drives to keep him from going rusty. He finished third in a round of the British F3000 series at Oulton Park early in the season driving a year-old Reynard-Ford behind Andrew Gilbert-Scott and Gary Brabham, and also ran at Le Mans in a Porsche 962 entered by Richard Lloyd Racing. They were inconsequential forays which proved very little.

He was good to work with — concise and perceptive in his comments about the car

A few weeks later he was thrown a lifeline from an unexpected source. The Japanese Mooncraft Formula 3000 team invited him to replace Ukyo Katayama who had been run ragged by commuting between Europe and Japan, attempting to take in championship programmes in both countries.

'He really wasn't up to all this travel and, in addition, had major language problems with our engineers,' remembers John Wickham, then Mooncraft's team manager. 'So we arranged a test session at Snetterton for both Damon and Perry McCarthy, both of whom lapped at much the same speed. But the sponsors liked the idea of Damon and we signed him for the rest of the season.' It was a rare occasion when being Graham's son definitely gave his career a leg-up.

'He was very good to work with,' said Wickham. 'Very concise and perceptive in his comments on the car. I think his F3 career had been a bit up and down, but I was impressed. He was certainly getting better and better by the time he drove for us.'

In 1990, things took another turn for the better when Damon accepted an invitation to contest the International F3000 Championship at the wheel of a Lola-Cosworth T90/50 entered by the Milton Keynes-based Middlebridge Racing organisation. Despite the new Lola being short of pre-season testing, he started on pole position three times, led five races and recorded two fastest laps. But that first F3000 victory eluded him.

One of Damon's most impressive performances came at Silverstone where he led commandingly for 16 of the 41 laps before stopping with electrical problems out on the circuit. It was therefore sad that a

Damon's Ralt-Toyota en route to second place in the prestigious Macau Grand Prix, the 'Monaco of the Far East' held annually through the streets of the Portuguese colony on China's mainland (LAT).

Expanding the knowledge. Hill graduated to Formula 3000 for a couple of races in the GA Motorsport Lola during 1988, but they were inconclusive affairs apart from adding to his experience (LAT).

The Footwork-backed Mooncraft F3000 car was hardly the most competitive tool in 1989, but it kept Damon's professional career afloat and impressed many observers who watched him doggedly struggling with the difficult machine (LAT).

certain national newspaper carried a story which claimed that he had inadvertently flicked off the ignition switch — rumours which were made all the more difficult to bear as the car fired up at the first attempt on its return to the paddock.

Hill finished the season by taking 13th place in the championship, an end result which in no way reflected the promise he had displayed. For 1991 he was invited to drive for Barclay Team EJR, effectively still the Middlebridge team using sponsorship provided by Eddie Jordan, the team owner hedging his bets by maintaining an F3000 interest at the same time as building his fledgeling Formula 1 team.

Years after that maiden test outing at Donington Park, having progressed through his three-year stint in F3, Damon had now come back into Eddie Jordan's orbit as a member of his Formula 3000 team. Yet it was another disappointing season, yielding Damon only seventh place in the championship. In the back of his mind, did the Irish team chief consider that Damon had that special spark?

'Very difficult,' says Eddie Jordan thoughtfully, talking to the author in 1996. 'One of the things which makes it difficult to make such an evaluation that perhaps we should say is that Damon was very, very similar to Martin Donnelly. Had it not simply been for the way the dice rolled, I think we might have chosen Damon above Martin as a Formula 3000 team-mate to Johnny Herbert or Jean Alesi in 1988/89.

'I would safely say that the way that Martin Donnelly progressed and matured, for me he was, without question, a potential World Champion. If you then analyse the situation between Hill and Donnelly, they were so close in their F3 days, then it shouldn't be a surprise that Damon is going so well.

'Secondly, Hill in 1990 with the Lola F3000 was very quick, but run on a very small budget, and that was one of the reasons that we were keen to attract him for 1991 for our F3000 team. That was a very complicated year for us, as we were unsure whether we could find the resources for the move to Formula 1, and so we didn't want to break away from Formula 3000 completely as it was our only source of income, our lifeline.

'So, in reality, I'm not sure as things turned out how much real attention Damon got from us in 1991, but he did a very good job under difficult circumstances. And, remember, he finished a strong third in the final race at Nogaro when Reynard loaned us a car.

'Damon is a very strong character, that's my feeling. Some people think he should be harder, but I think he's tough. But he wants to have a quiet life. I don't think he finds the adulation, the hype, very easy. He is a very private man. He dotes on his private life and his family. The fact that he eventually picked Ireland as a place to make his home suggested he was tempted by a good quality of life rather than perhaps maximising the financial situation as he might have done in some other places.'

Damon underlined his speed in F3000 during 1990 with this Middlebridge Racing Lola, but mechanical reliability proved difficult to sustain (LAT).

By the end of the 1991 season the nature of contemporary Formula 1 was becoming extremely complex. The previous year the Williams Grand Prix team had decided that the sheer volume of test and development work would justify the need for a dedicated test driver and Mark Blundell, one of Damon's old sparring partners from the Formula Ford days, was given the job. For 1991 Blundell accepted a full-time offer to drive for the Brabham-Yamaha team, creating a vacancy at Williams which Damon filled with alacrity.

Blundell would later reflect that things might have turned out very differently had he turned down the Brabham drive and stayed on as the Williams test driver. Mark, one of the most popular members of the British motor racing community, weighed his words with extreme care when asked in 1996 how he personally rated Hill.

'It's a difficult one, that,' he said. 'All I would say was that, from Formula Ford onwards, there were four or five guys who did most of the winning – Johnny Herbert, Bertrand Gachot, me and a couple of others. Damon was only an occasional winner but, as he has since proved, you need the complete package to achieve success.

'I would take nothing away from Damon and his achievements. But I don't think any of us would have any qualms about reflecting on what he achieved before he drove the Williams. We all know the score, Damon included.'

By the start of 1992, Hill's expertise in this test driving role was such that Frank Williams confirmed that he would be the team's official reserve driver. If illness or injury prevented Nigel Mansell or Riccardo Patrese from racing, then Hill would step into the breach.

Meanwhile, through 1991 Damon had also been trying to keep the momentum of his own racing career going in Formula 3000. Juggling the two roles was not always an easy task.

'After a session with the Williams FW14 during 1991, for example, I found it rather difficult to be objective with my own Formula 3000 car,' he explained. 'I would find that the brakes were not very effective, that there wasn't enough punch from the engine or that it didn't hold the road very well. It took me a certain amount of time to acclimatise when I made the transition.

'The first time I drove the FW14 I was like a kid in Santa's grotto. It took some time for me to come down to earth. I said to myself

The 1991 Formula 3000 season was Damon's last in this category with the EJR/Barclay Lola, a programme which Eddie Jordan freely admits didn't get the attention it deserved due to his own burgeoning F1 project. Hill's best result came in a loaned Reynard when he finished third at Nogaro late in the season (LAT).

"right, you're here to do a job, so stop dreaming that you're a budding World Champion. Just get into the car and do what you're told". In any case, my illusions didn't last very long. Everyone working with the car – engineers and mechanics alike – brought me very quickly back to reality!'

The business of being a test driver required a disciplined and accurate focus. Damon made a point of never regarding the exercise as an ego trip designed to flatter his status.

'I'm not asked to drive the best car in Formula 1 today for my own personal pleasure,' he explained in 1992. 'In fact, I am not asked to drive the car flat-out anyway. That wouldn't be of use to anyone. My job is to drive at a pace which allows the engineers to do their respective jobs, probably at around 95 per cent of the car's potential.

'A test session has nothing like the excitement or glamour of a Grand Prix. It's just a job to be done like many others. Even so, the work can be immensely fulfilling since I know that I am making my own individual contribution to the progress of the team. Each time a Williams-Renault wins, it's my win in a way as well.

'There is also considerable pressure, as there are times when I am carrying the responsibility for the entire research programme on my shoulders. If I was to make a mistake, like going off and damaging the car, we would have to start again from scratch. That could spell catastrophe by putting the development programme off schedule, or even jeopardising the remainder of the season.'

Yet Damon made no such slips. In fact, the more he tested, the more he impressed his employers. Adrian Newey, by then the Williams chief designer, explains that he noted that Damon seemed to have 'spare mental capacity' quite early in his career with the team.

Back in 1991 and 1992 when Hill was occupied piling up testing miles on the Williams FW14 and 14Bs, Newey quickly appreciated that he never forgot prior instructions to make those cockpit adjustments requested by the team during the course of a run:

'Some drivers would simply forget what you'd told them unless you reminded them with a pit board, but Damon was always very good in that respect'.

Blundell's career with the Brabham-Yamaha team lasted only a single season. At the end of 1991, the Japanese engine supplier decided to switch its support to the promising Jordan F1 team and Brabham, by now in a financially precarious position, had to switch to leased Judd V10 engines for 1992.

The Brabham team started the season with a driver line-up of Belgian F3000 star Eric van de Poele and feisty Italian girl driver Giovanna Amati. However, after failing to qualify for the first three races, Amati was stood down before the European season kicked off at Barcelona.

Brabham team chief Dennis Nursey had wanted to include Damon as a race driver from the start of the year, but financial necessity required that Amati should be signed. Hill took over for the Spanish race, by which time the team seemed to be balanced on a financial knife edge.

En route to the Circuit de Catalunya, the Brabham transporter was impounded at Le Perthus, on the Franco-Spanish border. The police were acting as the result of a court order obtained by a company called Pol Marketing which was claiming £30,000 said to be owing for the provision of the Brabham team's corporate hospitality at the previous year's French Grand Prix.

The transporter was only released when the team agreed to leave the spare Brabham BT60B as hostage against payment of the debt. That meant that Hill and van de Poele faced the added pressure of knowing that if they damaged their race cars, no back-up chassis would be available. As things transpired, Hill failed to make the cut by six places after Saturday's second qualifying session was rained out.

A fortnight later he missed qualifying for the San Marino GP by 1.2sec. At this race the Brabham team had been debarred from competing in Friday morning's free practice when technicians from John Judd's company removed the electronic control boxes from the

Desperate apprenticeship. Damon's F1 graduation came in 1992 at the wheel of the hopelessly uncompetitive and under-financed Brabham-Judd BT60B. His 11th place finish here in the Hungarian GP was the team's last outing before it went bust — 30 years since the first Brabham F1 car made its GP debut (LAT).

Graduation time. Damon at the wheel of the Williams FW15C which, as the team's test driver, he did so much to develop. Then he found himself contesting the 1993 World Championship in its cockpit after Nigel Mansell's switch to Indycars (LAT).

V10 engines to prevent them being fired up. Payment of the lease fees was overdue. The situation was resolved however and the team was allowed to continue limping along.

Then came Monaco and Damon faced all the emotional expectancy from the media. It was 34 years since Graham Hill had made his F1 debut through the streets of the Principality with a frail Lotus 12. On that unmemorable occasion, Graham's race finished when the car lost a wheel at the chicane.

Again, Damon failed to make the cut. 'When I see Nigel Mansell and Riccardo Patrese passing me out on the circuit, I feel terrible,' he confessed. 'It's very soul destroying, but I like to think there's a bit of me in that Williams FW14B.'

At Brabham the unrelieved gloom continued in the Canadian and French Grands Prix, but then came the British race at Silverstone where the cards would fall in Damon's direction at last. The Brabham team's dwindling budget had somehow run to funding slight improvements to the Judd V10 engines and to some aerodynamic modifications. In Friday qualifying, he managed 26th fastest time and his precious last place on the starting grid was preserved when steady rain fell throughout the Saturday afternoon session.

Come the race, Nigel Mansell delighted the 120,000-strong crowd with a brilliant flag-to-flag victory for Williams. Almost unnoticed in the crush, Damon got home in 16th place, four laps behind the winner. He also had a first-hand view of Mansell mania on the slowing down lap.

'I was right behind Mansell and thought we're not going to get out of here alive, because the place was just awash, just swarming with people,' he told *Autosport*. 'I nearly ran over six people. They didn't seem to know that there were other cars on the circuit, they just saw Nigel and leapt onto the circuit. It was very difficult. They were giving me a great big cheer, even though I was almost last.'

As Hill slogged round that final lap at Silverstone, he could hardly have imagined what a drama was bubbling up behind the closed doors of the Williams team. Nigel Mansell, poised on the glorious verge of his World Championship title, was locked in negotiations with the team for an extension of his contract into 1993. It was clear that these talks were not going well.

The 1992 Hungarian GP at Budapest saw Mansell finally clinch his title with a strong second place behind Ayrton Senna's McLaren-Honda. Damon slogged home 11th in what was the final finish ever posted by a Brabham F1 car. It was 30 years since his father had won the German GP at Nurburgring, the race in which Jack Brabham fielded a car bearing his own name for the very first time.

Now, more than a generation later, the Brabham team was teetering on the edge of oblivion. They failed to make it to the Belgian GP a fortnight later. It was the end of the road.

Meanwhile, Mansell had discovered that Frank Williams was set on signing Alain Prost to drive alongside him in 1993. Prost, who had taken a year's sabbatical after being fired by Ferrari one race prior to the end of the 1991 season, was determined to have a shot at a fourth World Championship crown.

Meanwhile, shrewdly judging the prevailing wind of contract negotiations, Riccardo Patrese snapped up the offer of a Benetton-Ford contract alongside Michael Schumacher for the 1993 season. But Mansell, who felt his status as newly crowned World Champion left him in an unassailable bargaining position, was not keen on Prost's imminent arrival. He had spent the 1990 season partnered alongside the Frenchman at Ferrari and hadn't enjoyed the experience. Prost, he reasoned, was a highly political animal.

Be that as it may, Williams was going to have Prost come hell or high water. With about 45 per cent of his team's overall £25 million operating budget being provided either by Elf, the French national oil conglomerate, or Renault — in the form of free engines and technical

Right *Focusing on the job. Damon's mother always reckoned that with his helmet on he looked startlingly like his father Graham, particularly the eyes* (LAT).

back-up – Frank was not going to bite the hands which fed him so generously.

The negotiations with Mansell spiralled out of control. Eventually they fell apart in the run-up to the 1992 Italian GP at Monza. Neither party would ever comment on the rumours that the reputed £8 million deal foundered on a point of trivia, namely the number of hotel rooms which would be available for the new World Champion's entourage at each race.

Nevertheless, it is clear that Williams forced Mansell into a decision by offering him a considerably lower figure than was originally put on the table. Mansell had evidently delayed making a decision on the earlier higher figure, seeking further assurances about Prost's future status in the team.

The crisis broke at Monza where, on race morning, Mansell marched into the media centre and announced that he would be retiring from F1 at the end of the season. Shortly afterwards, he confirmed that he would cross the Atlantic to drive a Newman/Haas team Lola-Ford Indycar the following season, effectively taking the seat vacated by Michael Andretti who had already signed an F1 contract with McLaren for 1993.

None of this drama immediately affected Damon, although it was clear that he was a possible candidate for the vacant Williams-Renault seat. It was by no means a certainty however. Although very familiar with the car, he lacked experience in the rough and tumble of Grand Prix action. Martin Brundle and Mika Hakkinen were both rated more likely candidates, but their chance came and went as Frank Williams considered each man – and rejected them both.

Damon kept alert to all the possibilities. The Ligier-Renault team was showing interest in his services, so he shrewdly invested £600 in a bucket shop ticket to get himself to the final race of the season in Adelaide. 'I'm going to stand in the back of the Williams garage, just to remind Frank I'm still around,' he grinned. 'And to talk to the Ligier team.'

Yet Frank Williams had certainly not forgotten him. Nor had Patrick Head, the Williams team's technical director who could clearly see the benefits in terms of continuity offered by promoting Hill to the full-

Main picture *Williams-Renaults ahead. Alain Prost leads Damon on the opening lap of the rain-soaked 1993 European GP at Donington Park, but Ayrton Senna's McLaren-Ford is already slicing past Karl Wendlinger's Sauber-Mercedes to take third place. The Brazilian ran rings round the two Williams drivers on that sodden afternoon (LAT).*

Inset *Painful moment. The Renault V10 engine in Damon's Williams FW15C expires spectacularly while he was leading the 1993 British Grand Prix at Silverstone. Had it survived, this would have been a fight to the finish with team-mate Alain Prost who was right on his tail (LAT).*

Keeping in trim. From the very start of his competition career, Damon has displayed a single-minded commitment to his physical fitness (Canon Williams).

time race team. Damon knew the ropes, and that was a matchless advantage he had over all the other candidates for this plum drive.

Early in December 1992, Damon Hill was summoned to Frank Williams's presence and duly drove down the M4 from his home in Wandsworth to the team headquarters, then at Basil Hill Road, Didcot. There, in Frank's spacious and airy office, he was told that he'd got the drive for 1993 alongside Prost, together with a retainer in the order of £300,000.

If Hill's own efforts had gained him a place on the launching pad, it was Frank Williams who had taken the decision to OK the lift-off. At 32 years of age, Damon was well and truly on his way up.

Going into the 1993 season, Hill would find himself happily well acquainted with the Williams-Renault FW15C which the team would use in its latest assault on the World Championship. Motor racing's governing body, the FIA, had decided the previous summer that tyre sizes would be reduced in the interests of safety.

In the pre-season tests, Hill was as quick, if not quicker, than Prost. But those who knew Alain well fully appreciated it would be wrong to read too much into these statistics. The Frenchman was a master at the art of keeping his powder dry for the Big Day.

Damon's maiden race for Williams was the South African GP at Kyalami where he qualified fourth behind Prost, Ayrton Senna's new

McLaren-Ford MP4/8 and Michael Schumacher's Benetton-Ford B193. During those official timed sessions, Damon's inexperience showed. He tended to get blocked in by slower cars and he still had to acquaint himself with the technique of using his tyres to best effect, a crucial factor as new rules limited all competitors to seven sets of tyres per race weekend.

Come the race, it was an inauspicious debut for the new boy at Williams. Tight on Senna's tail in second place going through the first ess-bend after the start, he spun wildly. Quite simply, he had got too close to the McLaren, lost aerodynamic downforce and, with it, control.

After regaining control, he settled down to run 12th before being bundled into a sand trap by Lotus new boy Alessandro Zanardi. Yet Damon remained philosophical. 'I made a great start, but I was right up to Ayrton's wing and it was really too much,' he reflected.

'I managed to recover and keep going, but it was very difficult to overtake out there. If I had not spun, I would not have been where I was (down the field) and would not have got into any other trouble.'

A fortnight later, the Formula 1 circus moved from the rolling backdrop of the South African veldt to the urban squalor of downtown

Concentration. In the pits watching the timing monitor in company with Williams chief designer Adrian Newey (centre) and Frank Williams (LAT).

Oh happy day. Damon speeding to an unchallenged victory in the 1993 Hungarian GP, breaking his F1 duck after a succession of disappointments (LAT).

Sao Paulo and the Interlagos circuit, venue for the Brazilian Grand Prix.

Understandably, Senna was hell-bent on winning this race in his own backyard, but the estimated 60bhp surplus enjoyed by the two Williams-Renault drivers ensured that his McLaren-Ford was kept back in third place in the final grid order.

Damon's confidence had in no way been dented by his experience at

Kyalami. In fact, he was champing at the bit to be allowed the chance to go out in the final session and take a tilt at Prost's fastest qualifying time. 'No Damon,' said Frank Williams firmly. 'I don't want you having the added pressure of having to start from pole position.' End of debate.

At the start Prost accelerated straight into the lead with Senna slipping ahead of Hill into second place. Not until lap 11 did Damon summon the confidence to outbrake the McLaren into the chicane beyond the pits, slipping neatly through to take second place. Senna watched with interest. 'I got the strong impression that he was sizing me up, seeing what I was like,' said Hill after the race.

Then a mid-race rain shower caught out Prost badly. He dodged away from the pit entrance at the last moment, confused by a garbled message over the radio, and spun off on a raging torrent of water going into the first turn, his slicks unable to cope with the conditions. Hill, who had made the change to rain tyres a lap earlier, survived to take the lead and, after the safety car was deployed to clear up the debris of Prost's Williams following its collision with Christian Fittipaldi's Minardi, Damon found himself in a sprint to the flag with Senna.

For five laps he stormed round at the head of the pack, even staying ahead of Ayrton after their second stops to switch back to slicks as the circuit dried out. But Senna wasn't to be denied in front of his home crowd, slamming through to take the lead on lap 42. Damon tried to keep up, but after getting into a big slide at the bottom of the hill beyond the pits, prudently settled for second. His first ever helping of championship points had earned him a place on the podium.

Senna could not believe it when Damon kept the door very firmly closed

However, if Hill thought that he'd seen rain in Sao Paulo, it was as nothing to the conditions experienced in the third round of the title chase, the European GP at Donington Park on 11 April, Easter Sunday. Again he qualified second, but again Senna displayed his legendary wet weather skills with a brilliant run to victory, storming through from fifth at the first corner to take the lead from Prost before the end of the opening lap.

To be fair, Prost refused to let go in the opening stages. As the track surface began to dry, he trimmed back Ayrton's advantage from 7.03sec at the end of lap four to 3.4sec before making a switch to slicks on lap 19, followed by a premature change back to wet rubber only three laps later.

Both Prost and Hill were struggling. Handicapped by some poorly judged rear wing adjustments made at their first stops, they were also beset by problems when it came to matching the engine revs correctly as the semi-automatic gearboxes changed down for the corners.

Hill finished the day a strong second ahead of Prost, but Frank Williams was critical of the Frenchman. 'It is obvious that Alain made a very clever tactical (first) change onto dry tyres, but threw it away with a vastly premature switch back to wets, and that was the rest of the race.

'It surprised me that a driver of Alain's experience should make those mistakes. All tyre changes were initiated and motivated by the driver. Any suggestion that anybody else made these decisions is untrue.'

Prost later admitted that he had already considered retirement the day after the Donington race, so it was unfortunate that Williams and

That's my boy. On the victory rostrum at Budapest, 1993. Father Graham would have loved it (LAT).

Taking a drink. Anticipating the future, perhaps? (LAT)

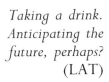

Renault chose to douse the flames of controversy with petrol rather than water, following the episode up with a press statement which, although trying to be conciliatory, made the parties involved look absurd.

But these problems were consigned to the back burner by the time the San Marino GP at Imola came round where Prost and Hill again buttoned up the front row of the grid only for a rain shower to intervene once again just before the start.

With the pack on deep-grooved rain tyres, Hill got the jump on Prost as the cars strung out round the long Tamburello left-hander, but if Senna thought that the new boy ahead would make room for him coming into the braking area for the uphill Tosa hairpin, he was very much mistaken.

The Brazilian couldn't quite believe it when Damon kept the door very firmly closed, extending his lead all the way round to complete the opening lap 1.8sec ahead. Ayrton thereafter pulled every trick in the book to keep Prost in third place, to such good effect that Hill was 8.6sec ahead when the Williams team leader finally managed to squeeze past the McLaren.

By this time the track was drying out and Damon waited until lap 11 before coming in for slicks. Although he got out of the pits just in the lead, Prost and Senna swooped past at the top of the hill beyond Tosa and he was suddenly back in third place. On lap 22, having got slightly off-line lapping Zanardi, Damon hit a wet patch and slid straight into the gravel trap at Tosa.

'I had been grappling with a slightly long brake pedal movement,' he later explained. 'Then, suddenly, the problem seemed to get worse and I slid off the circuit. I am extremely browned off.'

Those early races of 1993 had left Damon in a strange state of limbo as regards the perception of his abilities within the F1 community. He had the best car, but could he actually deliver the results? It looked as though the Spanish Grand Prix at Barcelona would provide an overwhelmingly affirmative answer to that lingering question.

Alain qualified on pole, but Damon beat him to the draw at the somewhat chaotic start, helped by an apparent wiring fault in the control mechanism of the starting lights which caused them to change from red to flashing orange, rather than the intended green.

Prost eventually got ahead, but Damon counter-attacked and was looking for a way past when his Renault V10 suffered a rare piston failure and he coasted into the pits with 40 of the race's 65 laps complete.

'A very disappointing end to the day,' he said. 'I was well in control of the situation, staying with Alain and watching every move he made and at the same time looking for opportunities without taking a big risk.'

Prost agreed that on this occasion he might well have been challenged. 'I think that if he (Damon) had been able to keep going at that pace, I would have been in trouble for sure,' he admitted frankly. 'The race was tiring and maybe one of my most difficult races physically. I don't usually have any problems, but I did today.'

Then came Monaco, and with it the nerve-wracking experience of a broken rear suspension wishbone which pitched Damon's Williams into a 170mph spin as he sped out of the tunnel on the approach to the chicane during Saturday's free practice session.

Amazingly, the car didn't touch the barriers, but it was certainly a worrying moment for the Williams team. Earlier during that same session a cracked lower suspension wishbone had been noticed on Prost's car and was duly replaced. Now both cars were again fitted with replacement lower rear wishbones prior to the start of first qualifying.

Prost grabbed pole position from Schumacher's Benetton-Ford and a bruised Ayrton Senna, nursing the legacy of a practice accident at Ste Devote. Hill was fourth and he held that position from the start, the pack running in grid order behind Prost. Unfortunately Alain incurred a 10sec stop-go penalty for jumping the start fractionally, a delay which handed Schumacher the lead until he stopped out on the circuit with an engine bay fire caused by an hydraulic fuel leak.

The battle for pole between the Williams drivers was simply electrifying

This left Senna in a position relentlessly to assert his advantage, steadily pulling away from Damon in the second half of the race to score an unmatched sixth Monaco victory. Hill survived being pitched into a spin by Gerhard Berger's Ferrari under braking for the Loews hairpin, displaying great presence of mind as he kept the Renault engine from stalling and continued to finish second.

Senna's victory finally eclipsed Graham Hill's record of five wins through the sunlit streets and Damon was quick to offer just the right words of praise for this momentous achievement:

'It is 30 years since my father's first victory here and I'm sure he would have been the first to congratulate Ayrton on breaking his record of five wins. It is a tribute to my father as much as to him that it has taken someone of Ayrton's calibre to do it.'

Senna could see that the words came from Damon's heart, quietly turned to him with a smile and shook his hand warmly. There was nothing else that needed to be said.

Damon took a third place in the Canadian Grand Prix at Montreal, then followed Prost dutifully home to second place in the French Grand Prix at Magny-Cours. Again the two Williams-Renaults were the class of the field in Alain's home race, so there was no point in their racing each other.

However, Damon achieved another significant milestone in France by qualifying on pole position for the first time in his career. By now he admitted he was learning important lessons from the great French champion, saying that the experience of operating as his team-mate had certainly been illuminating.

'It is a professional relationship,' explained Damon. 'You don't have to be friends with the people you work with, but you do need to get on with them. You must create the right environment whereby you get the most out of yourself and don't create any animosity – unless that's the way you want to work, but I don't like working like that.

'I like Alain, but I wouldn't count him as a friend of mine. I wouldn't presume to. I want to find out how I match up to him in real terms. His concentration over a race weekend is total and he barely spends a second without thinking what needs to be done, or what can be done, to win the race.'

Hill now headed home to Silverstone in a mood to win his home Grand Prix. More than that, he *believed* he could get the job done on a circuit with which he was totally familiar. But there was a lingering

Dynamic partner. Damon with Ayrton Senna prior to the start of the 1994 Grand Prix season. Most people believed Hill would be cast in a supporting role, but tragedy was lurking in the shadows (Renault Communications).

problem for the Williams team which was keeping its fingers crossed that the FIA would adjudicate favourably on a fuel sample taken from Prost's winning car at Barcelona.

Unfortunately, the FIA's decision was not expected until four days after the Silverstone race, forcing Alain to think in terms of the championship rather than any generous gesture in helping Damon. The battle for pole between the two Williams drivers was simply electrifying, but just when Hill felt he'd done enough to secure premier position in the line-up, Prost pulled that little bit extra out of the bag.

Patrick Head was left grinning fit to bust. 'That's what it should all be about,' he enthused. 'Two guys really getting stuck in and giving each other a bit of stick.'

Hill left the front row of the starting grid as if his life depended on it, accelerating into an immediate lead as the pack made for Copse corner. As at Imola, Senna's McLaren came rocketing through into second place, boxing out Prost. It was sad therefore that the Brazilian spent the first eight laps of the race pulling every dubious trick in the book in his efforts to keep Prost, his hated adversary, back in third place.

By the time Prost finally got ahead, Damon had built up an 8.1sec lead and was driving brilliantly. The crowd was hypnotised by the battle between the two Williams-Renaults. Hill's advantage fluttered – 8.2sec, 7.8sec, 8.0sec, 7.6sec – and by lap 28 Alain had edged his way to within 5.2sec of his team-mate. But still the outcome looked finely balanced, particularly with routine tyre stops still to come.

As things transpired, Hill got some bad breaks in traffic and the two cars resumed after their pit stops only 3.3sec apart at the end of lap 29. By lap 35, Alain was only 1.3sec adrift and it began to look as though the race might be slipping away from Damon. Then suddenly out came the safety car and the pack closed up into tight formation while Luca Badoer's abandoned Lola-Ferrari was moved from its parking place on the outside of Woodcote.

After three laps at reduced speed, the pack was unleashed again and Hill immediately opened out a 1.3sec advantage. But just as it seemed that the two Williams teamsters were about to become locked in battle for the lead, an exhaust valve on Damon's engine shattered and he rolled to a bitterly disappointed halt.

Prost reeled off the remaining 18 laps unchallenged to score an easy win, the 50th of his career, but he was quite aware that this was not the result the crowd had been praying for – he hardly acknowledged the chequered flag as he roared out of Woodcote for the last time.

'I don't really like winning in this ambience,' he admitted. 'I think Damon deserved to win here at home, but I also think I did a good job today.' The only consolation offered to Hill was the fact that the failure hadn't been his fault, which was confirmed by Renault Sport technical director Bernard Dudot after examining the engine in detail.

There was more good news for the Williams team the following week when the fuel samples from Barcelona were given the all-clear and Prost's Spanish GP success was no longer in danger. Yet Hill was beginning to wonder if he was ever destined to win a Grand Prix, a feeling made all the more acute as victory in the German GP at Hockenheim fell from his grasp a fortnight later after a rear tyre punctured with just over a lap to run.

Prost had been hit with yet another stop-go penalty early in the race for straight-lining the Ostkurve chicane, clearly to avoid an accident when he spied Martin Brundle spinning wildly under braking right behind him on the first lap.

This effectively put Alain right out of contention and, although he had closed to within 11sec of Hill with six of the race's 45 laps to run, there was clearly no way he could challenge the Englishman in the few miles left to the chequered flag.

On lap 39, Damon asked anxiously over the radio 'One-two or two-one?' – meaning did he have to relinquish the lead to Alain. He was reassured by a signal from his pit crew which read 'P1 OK.'

Coming out of the Osktkurve for the penultimate time, Damon's heart jumped as he noticed the puncture warning light flickering on his Williams dashboard. To begin with, he wasn't too worried, knowing that it sometimes came on if a driver was pushing hard because the tyre pressures sometimes drop a bit.

'I then felt the car oversteer suddenly as I came out of the chicane,' he recalled, 'but I was in fourth gear, accelerating up towards 130mph when the left rear tyre suddenly went. It must have been a sharp object – or something like that – going right through the tyre.'

Damon would have been forgiven a certain feeling of despair. Yet only three weeks later he raced to an unchallenged victory in torrid conditions at Budapest, finally breaking his F1 duck to win the Hungarian Grand Prix after a disciplined drive under no pressure but his own.

On this occasion Prost was forced to start from the back of the grid after his Renault engine refused to fire up as he made to start the final parade lap from pole position. Damon was thus allowed a trouble-free run to victory by over a minute from Riccardo Patrese's Benetton-Ford.

Yet the real pressure had come from within himself: 'I kept telling

Right *The lowest moment. Only a fortnight after Senna's fatal accident at Imola, Williams fielded just a single car for Damon in the Monaco Grand Prix. It was a crushingly painful weekend, made more emotional by the Brazilian flag fluttering respectfully above the Williams pit. Hill would crash out on the opening lap* (Darren Heath and ICN UK Bureau).

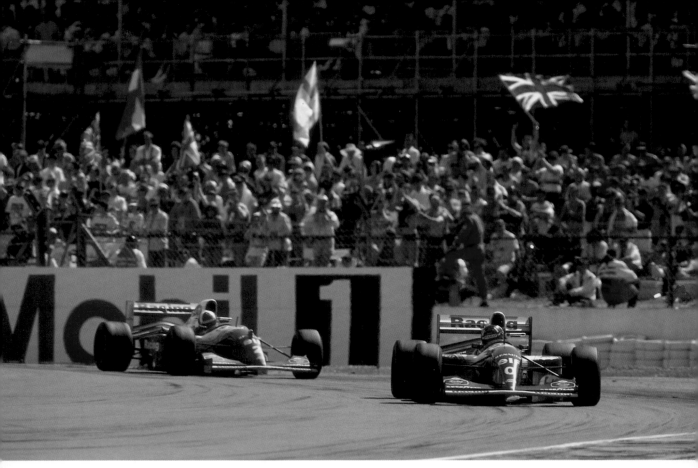

Golden moment. Damon would win the 1994 British Grand Prix at Silverstone after Michael Schumacher was black-flagged off the circuit. Here Hill laps his team-mate David Coulthard who finished sixth after stalling at the first – aborted – start and then had to take the restart from the back of the grid (Darren Heath).

myself it's not over until it's over, and I thought of my Dad and what he might have said to me to keep my concentration up. And if you knew my Dad, you know that just imagining him talking to me was enough to make me concentrate.'

Frank Williams joked that, having won his first race, Damon might well reel off victories in the next two or three as well. Nobody knew how serious that remark really was, yet the fact that Williams articulated those thoughts in public served as a reminder as to just how unpredictable the F1 business can be.

Amazingly, that's just what happened. Damon reeled off convincing victories in both the Belgian and Italian Grands Prix, both at the expense of his team-mate. It was payback time, but for Prost the real problem was not now out on the circuit. It was clear that Frank Williams was hell-bent on having Ayrton Senna in his team's line-up for 1994. And Alain felt about the Brazilian much the same as Mansell had felt about himself only 12 months earlier.

For Damon's part, that Monza success opened up the mathematical chances of winning the 1993 World Championship. But with three races still to go, he wasn't allowing himself to think in those terms. As it happened, he had problems firing up his Williams at the start of the Portuguese Grand Prix and it was his turn to start at the back of the grid.

'The external starter became dislodged on Damon's car,' explained Patrick Head, 'and we had some difficulty inserting it back into its aperture because of the failure of a little light bulb inside the shaft which is designed to help the mechanics locate the correct position.

'Eventually we got the engine fired up, but it was still quite cold and running rather erratically. In a couple more seconds, it would have been revving freely, but Damon flicked it into first gear and it stalled. By the time we reset the automatic gearchange and fired it up for the second time, the rest of the field was setting out on its parade lap.'

Hill stormed through to third behind Schumacher's Benetton and Prost, the Frenchman thereby clinching his fourth World Championship title. But the previous day Prost had announced his retirement from Formula 1 at the end of that season and, in the break which followed the Portuguese race and the Japanese Grand Prix, Williams confirmed that Ayrton Senna would in fact be partnering Hill in the team's line-up for 1994.

Hill had mixed emotions about driving alongside somebody with the Brazilian's forceful character: 'The job of a racing driver is not confined to circulating around the track. As a driver, I know that in order to get where I want I have to work for the team and within the team, so that might be to my detriment.

'I think he (Ayrton) is far and away the most complete and the fastest driver currently racing – or will be when Alain retires. He's head and shoulders, really, above everybody else.

'But I am not easily demoralised or crushed, so I am well prepared for that. I'm still on an upward climb in my F1 career and still have to learn a lot. Having someone like Ayrton as my team-mate will only add to my development.'

Senna quite clearly did not rate Damon as a threat to his own position, yet he picked his words with diplomatic care when asked by the British media to comment on his new partnership:

'Damon has won Grands Prix, he has been on pole position and led races. He has forced his way up in a natural way which gives all of us drivers a lot of confidence. He couldn't have a better start to his F1 career than one season with Alain and then a second season with me.'

Hill went on to complete the 1993 season with a fourth place in Japan and third at Adelaide, the final race of the season. He had done everything and more that had been expected of him and finished third in the World Championship.

'Damon's outstanding characteristic is his fierce determination,'

Left *On top of the world. Damon showers the champagne after his 1994 British GP victory, filling a gap in the family records with a triumph which had always eluded his father (Darren Heath).*

recalled Patrick Head. 'He seemed to have great depths of personal resource. Instead of wringing his hands and gnashing his teeth when things go wrong, he will sit down, go through all the available data, work it all out and go quicker the next day.'

As he set off for a winter holiday in the Caribbean with Georgie and their sons, Damon Hill might well have reflected that 1993 had really been a pretty good season, all things considered. In reality, this was the easy bit. The really serious Formula 1 challenge lay ahead. But much closer than he could ever have imagined.

Damon's relationship with Ayrton Senna was governed from the outset by the Brazilian's long-established reputation. The gifted, motivated Senna approached his motor racing with a passionate zeal which was almost religious in its intensity. He would do anything to win, and if that meant psychologically destroying his current team-mate, then so be it.

Hill purported to be unconcerned: 'What do people think Ayrton is going to do to me? Apply a Vulcan. mind grip or something? I appreciate that Ayrton is the benchmark for all F1 drivers, but there are a number who think they can beat him.

'I believe I will start the coming season with a very good chance of the title. I'm not saying it is going to be easy, but the opportunity is there and I intend to do all I can to realise my ambitions.'

The 1994 Formula 1 regulations had been formulated to swing the emphasis back towards driver skills after a period of intensive technical development. Computer controlled active suspension, anti-lock braking and traction control systems were all banned. While such changes to the rules might reasonably have been expected to favour the dynamic Senna, the new Williams FW16 proved rather difficult to drive on its debut in the Brazilian GP at Interlagos.

A measure of its shortcomings could be gauged from the fact that Senna over-drove wildly and spun off in the closing stages of his home race as he sought to close the gap on Michael Schumacher's winning Benetton-Ford B194, clearly the class of the new field.

Hill finished the Brazilian race in second place, wrestling with a head cold for much of the weekend, and then both Williams drivers failed to finish the Pacific GP at Japan's new TI Aida circuit. Senna was nudged off the road at the first corner by Mika Hakkinen's McLaren and Hill succumbed to engine failure while running second to Schumacher later in the race.

All this was detail. The epicentre of the 1994 Formula 1 World Championship season would prove to be the weekend of the San Marino Grand Prix at Imola. This was to be motor racing's equivalent of President Kennedy's assassination, a three-day spell which would remain etched in the memory for all time.

In Saturday's qualifying session, the Austrian novice Roland Ratzenberger was killed in a horrifying high-speed accident at the wheel of his Simtek-Ford. It was the first Formula 1 fatality at a race meeting for 12 years. But the horror was not over. The following day, leading the opening stages of the race, Senna's Williams plunged off the circuit at 190mph on the entrance to the flat-out Tamburello corner just beyond the pits. Ayrton, the sport's leader, suffered serious head injuries from which he succumbed a few hours later.

The Formula 1 fraternity was propelled into a state of freeze-frame numbness. The race was naturally red-flagged to a halt, eventually to be restarted almost an hour later. In truth, it had been something of a gamble to allow Damon back into the competition as the team had no way of knowing whether or not Ayrton's accident had been caused by a mechanical failure.

Patrick Head's first decision had been to uncouple the power steering mechanism on Hill's car, thinking perhaps that some sort of pressure drop-off within the system might conceivably have had something to do with Ayrton's loss of control. Damon raced hard to sixth place, despite a delay to replace a nose section damaged against a rear wheel of Schumacher's Benetton.

Then it was back to England. Damon, Georgie and many of the Williams team personnel were in a state of shock as they stumbled aboard the charter flight at Bologna airport for the journey back to Gatwick late in the evening of 1 May 1994. Yet Hill found time to compose a tribute to his dead colleague:

'For all his concerns about safety, he never played safe in the cockpit. He performed at one hundred per cent all the time and for that he commanded admiration from every driver. I will never forget my short period working with him and consider myself immensely privileged to have been a team-mate.'

As the Williams team returned to the Didcot factory there were floral tributes to Senna spilling out along the roadside. The Brazilian's wrecked FW16 had been impounded by the authorities pending an investigation, and this spectre of concern would underpin the team's thoughts as they steeled themselves to prepare for the relentless grind of the championship battle ahead.

The gaping void left by Senna was something which touched every person involved in the sport, but it impinged on Damon Hill probably more than any other individual. He now found himself propelled from a significant role in the supporting cast to number one player. Like his father before him who had battled to restore morale at Lotus after the death of Jim Clark in 1968, Damon faced the task of trying to raise spirits within the shattered Williams team. It was time to rise to the occasion and, despite his relative inexperience, Damon responded magnificently.

The Monaco Grand Prix was the next race on the calendar. It passed in a ghastly blur, made worse by another practice accident, this time to Sauber team driver Karl Wendlinger. The Austrian was taken to hospital where he languished in a coma for 18 days. Thankfully, he recovered.

Everybody's nerves were taut. Williams fielded one car, Damon qualifying fourth and then crashing out on the opening lap. 'The biggest responsibility for me is to shoulder the responsibility for the team,' he said. 'The whole thing is awful, a very sorry situation. The sooner we get away from Monaco and back to some semblance of normality, the better it will be.'

I'm privileged to have raced alongside the top three guys of the past ten years

Yet there were other worries on the horizon. To put it mildly, the Renault Sport management was getting an attack of the jitters. Unimpressed by Hill's Monaco debacle, they now signalled their willingness to bankroll a return to Williams by Nigel Mansell. The 1992 World Champion had enjoyed a great season to win the 1993 Indycar Championship, but now the Newman/Haas Lola-Fords were struggling. Mansell was receptive to a deal.

In the meantime, Damon was faced with a new team-mate for the Spanish GP at Barcelona, the young Scottish Formula 3000 graduate David Coulthard, who was also the Williams test driver.

The ghosts of Imola were far from exorcised. In practice at Barcelona, Andrea Montermini's Simtek-Ford crashed heavily on the final corner before the pits. It looked worse than it was. I walked down to the paddock from the press room to investigate. Behind the Williams transporter I was confronted by a wild-eyed Hill. 'Montermini?' he asked. I didn't quite know what he was getting at. 'He's dead,' he stated, and walked away.

I knew that wasn't the case, but somehow this didn't seem the moment to enter a debate with Damon. I was speechless. Later Hill was more relaxed and grinned sheepishly as he recounted our confrontation. But it was an indication of the huge tensions still felt within the F1 community that the accident should have elicted such a hair-trigger response.

Hill won the Spanish Grand Prix. He only went ahead after Schumacher's Benetton had gearbox troubles, but few victories have been harder achieved. It was a symbolic success which put Williams back in the winning mind-set. The fact that the FW16 chassis was still not the best machine out there seemed, for the moment, an issue of secondary importance.

The Renault Sport management fawned over Damon at his moment of triumph in a sickening display of ingratiating disingenuity. It was less than a fortnight since they had paraded their reservations about Hill. But now they were all over him like a rash.

Meanwhile, Renault was inching towards a deal with Mansell. He would be paid £900,000 per start for racing in the French, European, Japanese and Australian Grands Prix. Damon, earning nickels and dimes by comparison, could only be consoled by the challenge of trying to beat, fair and square, the man whose place he had taken at Williams barely 12 months earlier.

Meanwhile, Coulthard who had made his debut in Spain, was fielded as Damon's team-mate for the Canadian GP at Montreal. There the young Scot briefly ran ahead of his more senior colleague in the opening stages until cramp intervened in his right foot. Eventually, the Williams pits signalled that David should let Damon past. Hill finished second, 28sec behind Schumacher. He was slightly miffed.

'I understand the competitive nature of F1,' he conceded, 'and the fact that there's no love lost between team-mates, but it is, after all, supposed to be a team sport.

'I was getting a bit cheesed off (sitting behind Coulthard) because I knew I could go quicker, but even if I'd managed to get past him earlier, I don't believe I could have caught Michael.'

Schumacher now went into the French Grand Prix with 56 points to Hill's 23 and all eyes were firmly focused on Mansell's return to the F1 fold. Yet Damon was confident.

'I view it as an opportunity,' he claimed. 'I've had a fantastic opportunity to race alongside Alain, Ayrton and now Nigel as well, so that really completes the top three guys of the last 10 years. Not many people can say that, so I'm very privileged. It's an opportunity for me again to learn as much as I can and to see how I compare.

'If he beats me, then it shows that I haven't done a good enough job and I'll have to do a better one if I am going to stay in Formula 1. That's the bottom line.'

In fact, Damon did brilliantly. He outqualified Mansell to take pole position, then chased off after Schumacher's winning Benetton which came through to lead at the start like a dragster from the second row of the grid. Michael won again from Damon. Mansell retired when the gearbox hydraulics failed.

By this stage in the season, there was a worrying sub-text developing as a rider to the overall picture. Schumacher's rivals had convinced themselves that his succession of excellent starts indicated that his Benetton was fitted with some sort of illegal launch control system. Eventually the FIA would clear the team of any malpractice, but Schumacher remained at the centre of controversy for the balance of the season.

At the height of the downpour at Suzuka during the 1994 Japanese GP, the safety car was deployed to slow the pack. Here Hill trails round in second place behind Michael Schumacher's Benetton before going through to score one of the very best wins of his short career (Darren Heath).

At Silverstone, where Damon again qualified on pole position brilliantly in front of his home crowd, Michael's day ended when he was black-flagged off the circuit, and later excluded from the results, for overtaking Hill on the pre-race parade lap. In addition, Michael and the Benetton team were summoned before the FIA World Motor Sport Council which increased the £25,000 penalty imposed by the British GP stewards to £500,000, added to which Michael was suspended for two races.

This decision cruelly distorted the pattern of the 1994 World Championship battle. Although Schumacher's removal from the equation enabled Damon to storm to victory in the British Grand Prix, it was somehow a hollow win. The fact remained that he had yet to beat Michael fair and square.

This unsatisfactory season continued to grind along. Damon threw away victory in the German GP by colliding with Ukyo Katayama's fast starting Tyrrell on the opening lap. He wound up eighth on a day when Schumacher succumbed to engine problems. Then he was second to Michael in Hungary, but won at Spa only after the Benetton ace was disqualified for excessive wear on the wooden composite 'plank', a requirement for all Grand Prix cars in the wake of the Senna accident as part of a package of measures designed to slow lap times.

Schumacher had naturally appealed the decision to suspend him for two races, but the appeal was rejected immediately after the Spa race and the German now faced the prospect of sitting out both the Italian and Portuguese Grands Prix. If Damon was to have a chance of the title, he had to win these races. It put him under pressure of a different kind, but he did the job brilliantly.

Damon displayed a ruthless side to his character during this period. Prior to Monza, he asked the Williams management if David Brown, the team's senior engineer, could be switched to work on his car. The change was agreed, but John Russell, Damon's engineer ever since the start of 1993, was badly put out, as much by the way in which he was notified as by the decision. Williams insiders believed that Damon handled the split in a rather self-absorbed and tactless manner. Perhaps he was simply learning that a ruthless edge is a pre-requisite in the repertoire of any top F1 driver.

> **It's a daft attempt to destabilise me — he'll have to try better than that**

His talent behind the wheel was growing apace. Patrick Head, for one, was generous in his praise. 'I do think that Mansell's presence at Magny-Cours helped in a way in that, while I don't think for one moment he pinpointed any particular problem with the car, his views were similar to Damon's at a time when I think Damon was beginning to wonder whether it was the car, or him, or whatever.

'You've only got to watch Damon out on the circuit to realise that those people who say he's like his father — all determination and not much skill — are talking rubbish. He is a very skilful driver and I don't think we've seen what ultimate level he will achieve yet.'

Hill went into the European Grand Prix at Jerez only a single point behind the returning Schumacher. In the run-up to that particular race, Schumacher had made some waspish remarks to the effect that Hill was a second class contender. But Damon shrugged them aside with lofty indifference.

'I think it's a bit of a half-baked attempt to destabilise me, and he'll have to try better than that if he wants to do it,' said Hill with a rare degree of assurance. 'I'd rather not drag the championship down in that way by trying to diminish the reputation of the opposition. And I think it's sad that F1, for far too long, has arrived in that situation with the two protagonists seemingly hating each other's guts.

'That is sad for the sport, sad for F1, and especially so in a season where we've lost a great champion in Ayrton. I think Michael's remarks are ill-conceived and immature. But I wouldn't say there is any animosity between us. He's a young man and he has not been in this position before. Neither have I, but I think, I hope, that I can carry myself through this with some dignity and not resort to undermining the reputation of fellow competitors.'

Disappointingly, at Jerez Hill had to be content with second place after a glitch with the refuelling rig threw his pit stop strategy badly off course. A shame, because he had led Schumacher confidently in the opening stages when the final outcome had seemed too close to call. Schumacher had now opened out a five point lead with only two races still to go.

Then came the event at which Damon Hill finally stamped his identity on the Formula 1 community and grew, in effect, from adolescence to Grand Prix manhood. In the Japanese Grand Prix at Suzuka he kept control of the race on a near-flooded track surface in torrential rain — and beat Michael Schumacher into second place by 3.3sec.

Hill had only a single refuelling stop and surged past into the lead when Schumacher made the second of his stops with only 10 laps left to run. It was the most remarkable challenge of his career so far. In truly appalling conditions, he had to listen to his pit crew on the radio link advising him that Schumacher was nibbling away at his advantage.

On lap 43 the gap was 12sec, then 10.1, 8.3, 7.0, 5.2 and 4.2. With one lap to go Hill was 2.4sec ahead, but for Schumacher the game was up. On the final lap Damon actually opened out another second and crossed the line 3.3sec in front of his arch-rival's Benetton. He was now a single point behind Michael with only one race to go. And everything to play for.

One man who was enormously impressed by Hill's performance at Suzuka was Niki Lauda, the retired triple World Champion who now acted as a consultant to the Ferrari Formula 1 team. Niki knew more than most about the dangers of racing in the wet, having pulled out of the rain-soaked 1976 Japanese Grand Prix and lost the title battle to James Hunt as a result.

'When you think what he was doing at Suzuka, well, I would have shit my pants, to be honest,' he admitted with startling candour. 'If I had to drive in those conditions for the World Championship it would have been easier to say, well, I just don't care. But both he and Schumacher motivated themselves in an extraordinary way and Damon really did an incredible job. And I can tell you, I *know* what it means to drive in those sort of conditions.

'So, if you had to compare Damon and Michael on the strength of Suzuka only, you could really say Damon is as good as Schumacher. Over the season, I would say the record favours Schumacher. But they are very even now and Damon has caught up on the job.

'I really believe that . . .'

A second
place habit

By any objective standards, Damon Hill's victory in the 1994 Japanese Grand Prix was an outstanding achievement. To have withstood such consistent pressure from Schumacher in such appalling weather conditions not only raised the spirits of the Williams team, but also left Hill's German rival seriously wondering whether the World Championship might actually slip away from him at the last moment.

Yet if Damon hoped such a victory would dramatically raise his stock with the Williams management, this was not quite the case. Frank Williams and Patrick Head may have outwardly regained their own personal equilibrium after the Senna tragedy six months before, yet inwardly they felt the team was still in limbo to a very large degree.

Any analytical assessment of Hill's worth was coloured by the fact that Williams, indeed the sport as a whole, had lost its leader at Imola. Factors like Nigel Mansell bouncing back into the equation, allied to the complicated negotiations with David Coulthard about an extension of his contract, blurred their priorities.

One got the impression that Damon was still regarded as the tea boy who'd now been promoted to a place in the executive dining room. But, deep down, he was still the tea boy in their minds.

More specifically, harsh words had been exchanged between Head and Hill during practice at Suzuka after Damon had apparently had some difficulty getting up to speed through a couple of individual corners. The two men examined the telemetry traces, after which Head, perhaps thinking aloud, made it clear that he felt the problem was in the cockpit. Damon was momentarily lost for words. His consequent indignation further fuelled the worries he had about his position at Williams. And the worries continued despite his victory in the race.

On his arrival in Adelaide a week later, almost on the eve of the title shoot-out, Damon decided to play a strong card to the media.

'I'm pretty disgusted with some of the things which have gone on,' he bristled. 'I feel that they (Williams) have not contributed to making me feel that the team is behind me to win the championship.

'I have been in negotiation with them about my contract. I do have a contract; they have taken up their option on my services for next year, but I reckon I am a lot better than my contract says I am. The dispute is about the team recognising what you feel yourself to be worth.

'I have won nine Grands Prix. This year I have had to carry the role of number one driver in only my second season in F1. I'm one point off the championship lead with one race to go.'

Even before the Adelaide race it was almost inconceivable that Hill would not drive for Williams in 1995. In truth, it seemed likely that taking such an apparently outspoken stance was part of the process of hyping himself up into the sort of high pressure situation which brings out the best in him.

Fleetingly, there was speculation that he might switch teams. McLaren was mentioned, but while their team chief Ron Dennis was non-committal, he made some shrewd points about Damon's overall temperament:

'The fact that he didn't make a mistake at Suzuka speaks volumes for his character, but he doesn't seem to come across when he's out of the

Crunch day. The pack in full flight away from the starting grid at the 1994 Australian GP with Nigel Mansell's pole position Williams (No. 2) dutifully moving out of the way to let Schumacher and Hill get on with their World Championship battle (Darren Heath).

Hill had Schumacher seriously ruffled in Adelaide, but their nose-to-tail battle ended in tears when they collided seconds after the Benetton driver brushed a wall (ICN UK Bureau).

car, and I think he's as frustrated by that as he is with anything else.

'He craves recognition. I think his placid character doesn't go with his results. If his character was slightly more vivacious or sparkling, perhaps he would be held in higher esteem.'

For a while, it looked as though Schumacher was feeling the pressure at Adelaide. He crashed heavily on Friday morning, but eventually qualified second behind Williams returnee Nigel Mansell. Damon finished the first session third fastest, this being his eventual place on the starting grid as Saturday's second qualifying session took place on a wet circuit.

The build-up on race day morning was heavy with tension. Williams insiders were privately worried that Hill hadn't managed to bag a place on the front row, but at least Damon knew that Mansell would help his championship challenge. Nigel had pledged to get out of the way and let the two title protagonists get on with it.

Schumacher, for one, wasn't about to take Hill for granted. On the starting grid, the Benetton team leader gambled by reducing his car's aerodynamic downforce in the interests of straight line speed. It was a decision which would come within a few yards of costing him the World Championship.

'This is the Big One!' screamed the indefatigable Murray Walker to bleary-eyed British TV viewers as the pack completed its formation lap in the small hours of an autumn morning back in the UK. Red lights, green light and suddenly they were away in a wall of sound, Schumacher's Benetton already pulling level with Mansell's pole Williams as they jostled into the tight chicane only a few hundred yards away from the grid.

Nigel took a quick glance in his mirrors, saw Damon coming up as well, and neatly sidestepped his team-mate, moving over to the far right of the circuit to allow him through. By the end of the opening lap, Schumacher was a stupendous 2.1sec ahead of Hill, but that was as good as it got.

Both Michael and Damon were running on the same three-stop refuelling strategy and, by the end of the second lap, Hill had pulled up to only 0.4sec behind the leading Benetton. Nor was he hanging on by the skin of his teeth, but seriously challenging Schumacher for first place. For Michael, the penny suddenly dropped that he had a fight on his hands.

The two leading cars were totally embroiled in their own private battle, blowing the opposition away like never before. Damon was soon lapping within a few tenths of his own third place qualifying lap time and, with only 10 of the race's 81 laps completed, had opened an 18sec gap over Mika Hakkinen's third place McLaren-Peugeot.

Damon's first race of 1995 ended in disappointment when his Williams FW17 spun out of the lead in Brazil when its rear suspension broke (ICN UK Bureau).

At the end of lap 18 the atmosphere in the pit lane was electrifying as Michael and Damon came in for their first refuelling stops. Schumacher was ahead as they tore back into the fray, but there were increasing signs that Hill was getting the upper hand when it came to slicing through the slower traffic.

That last-minute decision to reduce the Benetton's downforce was making life lurid for Schumacher as he grappled with a touch more oversteer than he would have liked. Suddenly, mid-way round lap 36, the German ace made what looked like the vital slip.

Coming out of a medium-speed left-hander, the Benetton slid wide and glanced the concrete retaining wall. Crucially, though, Damon didn't witness this excursion having dropped back a few lengths, and was out of sight of his rival. All he saw was Michael coming back onto the grass.

Adelaide was absolutely his finest race — he was a man on a mission

'I thought, "hello, you've slipped up there,"' reflected Hill afterwards. 'But I thought his car was OK. Only when I later looked at the video was it clear that his right-rear suspension was pretty damaged and would have put him out of the race.

'Of course, it's easy if you want to look back in time. In retrospect, I would have let him go.'

For the next five seconds, the outcome of the 1994 World Championship was balanced on a knife edge. As Schumacher was apparently recovering, Damon saw his chance and dived for the inside going into the next right-hander. Michael pulled across him, the Benetton vaulted up onto two wheels as it rode over the Williams's left front corner, slammed down onto the track and slid straight into the tyre barrier on the outside of the turn. Schumacher was out.

Desperately hoping that his Williams could be repaired, Damon limped back to the pits. But there was nothing to be done. The left front top wishbone on the FW16 had been bent beyond repair. Hill sat glowering in the cockpit for several minutes, absorbing the disappointment, then he climbed out and strode into the Williams team office. He immediately telephoned Georgie, who'd been watching the action unfold on television 8000 miles away in Britain.

It was all history now. Schumacher made some self-conscious observations which amounted to back-tracking over his previous remarks which had called Hill's talent into question. Almost as a footnote, Nigel Mansell won the race in the other Williams-Renault, but it was not a success calculated to secure his full-time return to the team in 1995. David Coulthard would, after all, eventually be confirmed as the second driver.

It fell to Patrick Head to sum up Hill's efforts in Adelaide. 'It was absolutely Damon's finest race,' he said firmly. 'He was a man on a

Arch-rivals, sad day. Schumacher and Hill face the media at Imola on the first anniversary of Ayrton Senna's death (Darren Heath).

mission and, had it not been for the accident, I have no doubts that he would have got the job done.'

Hill flew back to London in the role of gracious loser. The FIA examined all the available evidence surrounding the collision and decided there were no grounds for further action. Damon remained stoic, declining to be drawn into any potential slanging match.

His performance had also endeared him to a wider public. Their votes ensured that he beat runner Sally Gunnell into second place to win the 1994 BBC Television Sports Personality of the Year award. In so doing, he joined Britain's first World Champion Mike Hawthorn, in addition to John Surtees, Jackie Stewart and Nigel Mansell, as priviliged recipients of this exclusive accolade.

'I started the season with the ambition of winning the World Championship,' said Hill after receiving the award from Chris Chataway, 'and this award will help fire my determination to realise that aim in 1995.'

Meanwhile, there was still the knotty question of finalising the details of Damon's new contract. Hill had originally been promoted to the F1 front line on what amounted to an extension of his original testing contract, as a result of which his basic pay for 1994 was probably less than £500,000.

Damon scored a great victory in the 1995 San Marino GP but he had to work hard for it in heavy traffic (ICN UK Bureau).

Damon felt this wasn't enough, particularly in view of Renault's willingness to bankroll Mansell's return to the team in 1994 for a fee of around $1 million (£770,000) per race. The disparity was obvious and, after a few more weeks of negotiation, Frank Williams hammered out a deal which went some way towards correcting that anomaly.

An official bulletin issued by the team confirmed the position. It read: 'The original deal was done when Damon was our test driver and in two years he has risen to the point where he is a World Championship contender. His situation has changed dramatically and Frank Williams has now rewarded Damon by giving him the financial recognition he deserves. From a Williams point of view, there was never any doubt that he would be driving for us next year and we exercised the option on his rolling contract with four races of the season still to go.'

A few weeks before the start of the 1995 World Championship season, I was, in my role as *Autocar* magazine's Grand Prix editor, fortunate enough to be invited to conduct an exclusive interview with Damon during a Williams team test at Estoril. The chance to spend an evening chatting over dinner with an F1 star is something to be prized, as much for the insight it offers into their mood as for what is actually discussed.

This convivial evening took place in a fish restaurant in the nearby port of Cascais, a fashionable resort for the rich and famous as photographs on the wall above our table of such disparate characters as the Duke of Windor and Mick Jagger testified.

Damon was relaxed, upbeat and amusing company. We were also joined by Patrick Head whose booming tones recalled, for no particular reason, the great days of 1973 when you could actually see Ronnie Peterson's Lotus 72 sliding all the way around Woodcote corner during the British Grand Prix at Silverstone.

Over the three months since Adelaide, Hill had found himself propelled from the position of mildly successful Grand Prix driver to a sporting superstar in the eyes of both media and public. He relished recounting the strange ways this new-found celebrity status had made itself felt.

'I was queuing for a carton of popcorn at a Phil Collins concert,' he said, 'and suddenly I heard this voice beside me say "You wuz robbed!"'

Damon had turned and smiled at the fan, who continued: 'You wuz robbed. I got it before Murray did. The guy just turned into you.'

Damon tried not to be rude. 'Yes, yes,' he replied, all the time thinking *come on, give me the popcorn* . . .

His new-found pal was now into his stride. 'He's good, isn't he, that Robbie Coltrane?' Hill froze. 'I know who you mean,' he replied, deadpan, trying not to laugh.

'Oh no,' said the friend. 'I got it all wrong. *David* Coltrane.' Damon grabbed the opportunity to make good his escape.

It was a far cry, he reflected, from a similar moment in Richmond Park the day after he won the 1993 Hungarian Grand Prix. Hill was walking there with his family when a passer-by simply smiled, said 'nice drive yesterday' and hardly broke his step.

'It was all that needed to be said,' he remembered with satisfaction. 'But that aspect is now different. I will go somewhere and can see, out of the corner of my eye, somebody approaching me.

'It goes through your head "oh, I don't want to be disturbed right now" but you can't turn people away who are coming up to say "you were brilliant last year and you was robbed."'

So how had Hill changed? Why did he think that the 1995 season would be different? Well, for a start, it certainly seemed from his demeanour that he was under rather less pressure than in 1994. Even though he was clearly taking nothing for granted, a mood of rock-hard confidence seemed evident just beneath the surface.

'I'm more comfortable with the whole situation,' he said, 'but you can never afford to relax. Every year you think "well, I've got the record to back up my credentials," but in this business, every year you are tested. You are only as good as your last race; that old adage really does hold true.

'Nobody is going to give you any credit if you don't deliver results on the day. That's always the niggling, motivating thing. It's no good saying "well, I wasn't quick today, but I won a few Grands Prix – I was quick last year." That's history!'

Damon also acknowledged that, as he became more accustomed to winning, the challenge of driving a Grand Prix car competitively seemed to change into a kind of mental slow motion.

'This may just be because you've managed to confirm to yourself what you feel you already know,' he mused. 'In the past few days here (at Estoril) I've felt really comfortable in the car. I don't mean physically, but mentally. I've been happy with the (new Williams) FW17.

'I think I know what I'm doing. The changes we have made (to the car) have been the right ones and these things seem to build in your mind the idea that you know your job.

'I've always felt I knew my job in terms of managing racing cars. It's just that in Formula 1 there are added pressures. You're at the sharp end of the business. The job is a bit more difficult than in the junior formulae when you buy a brand new off-the-shelf Lola, or whatever.'

Even more crucially than his own personal confidence, he felt that

Hill's Williams is serviced at one of its routine refuelling stops during the 1995 Spanish GP. He looked on course for second place behind Schumacher . . . (Darren Heath)

. . . but hydraulic failure on the final lap dropped him to fourth and he parked his Williams just beyond the finishing line (Darren Heath).

the 1994 season had finally earned him total acceptance within the Williams enclave.

'If you consider the history of Williams, they've had some great drivers who were of the same generation as Frank and Patrick in the early days,' he ruminated, 'and in the past 10 years they've had World Champions or front-running drivers from other teams. I have had to be aware of that fact.

'Last year I felt that I could assume the role of number one, but that was difficult for me to do within the team because I had no credentials to warrant that claim. I think, emotionally, I wanted to say "Look, Frank, if you want me to do it, and you want to get behind me, I can do it".

'But there was an understandable ambivalence and worry. I don't want anybody to think that I saw Ayrton's death as an opportunity – not at all – but I was the guy on the spot, and I felt that I could take the challenge to Michael.

'Coming as I did from the role of test driver to being regarded within the team as someone who has matured is quite difficult. Familiarity breeds not quite contempt, but perhaps blinds people who are close to the changes in another person.

Man under pressure.
Damon keeps his
thoughts to himself
(Darren Heath).

Damon worked hard
to qualify his
Williams FW17
superbly on pole
position for the 1995
Monaco Grand Prix
(Darren Heath).

'It can be rather like parents who don't accept that their children have grown up. It's not totally the case with Williams, but I think there is an element of it. Not long ago I was the test driver, now I've grown into a Grand Prix winner, still working with the same group of people.'

Most F1 observers considered that Williams entered the 1995 season with the best technical package. It was the team's sixth year with Renault and, although their key rivals Benetton had switched to share supplies of the French engines, Damon and his team-mate David Coulthard were both confident that they could start the first race in a winning position.

The latest Williams FW17 was a brand new design to conform with further revised F1 technical regulations which had been introduced in the wake of the Senna tragedy. For the second half of 1994, all the teams had been forced to adapt their existing cars, but now, with further rules added in an attempt to reduce lap speeds, Williams decided to kick off with a completely clean sheet of paper.

Damon had to avoid getting into any psychological battles with his arch rival

'Some parts of the car were not really much affected by the regulation changes and some were heavily affected,' explained Adrian Newey, the Williams chief designer. 'Given the amount of time available from when we started researching the car from the new regulations, it was a question of intelligent guesswork, of trying to judge which areas to concentrate on.' Among the many changes incorporated in Hill's own new car was a slightly higher steering wheel position. This was to get it further away from the brake pedal and provide more room for his size 11 feet!

For Damon, the off-season had been a time to sit and consider what was required to beat Michael Schumacher. You could tell that the Englishman was still smarting over the way in which the 1994 championship had been resolved, but he knew only too well that Schumacher regarded F1 racing as a mind game as much as anything else.

So not only did Damon have to keep control on the track, capitalising on the FW17's performance advantage for as long as possible while Benetton played catch-up, but he also had to avoid becoming embroiled in any psychological battle with his great rival.

The season began with the Brazilian GP at Sao Paulo's Interlagos circuit where every competitor expressed deep concerns about the bumpy nature of the track surface. Coulthard was still suffering badly from the after-effects of tonsilitis and qualified third behind Hill and Schumacher, Damon doing an excellent job to beat Michael to pole position.

However, just before the start of the race both Williams and Benetton encountered a major problem. The FIA, motor racing's governing body, had introduced new rules for 1995 which required teams to lodge samples of their fuel in advance of a specific race. This would allow checks to be carried out at the individual races where the 'fingerprint' of the approved fuel could be matched against a sample taken from the car in the pit lane.

Samples were duly taken from Schumacher's Benetton and Coulthard's Williams at Interlagos and found not to match the fingerprint. This news was communicated to the teams concerned only on the morning of the race – even though the samples had been taken after Friday's first qualifying session.

The implications were clear. Since there was only a single Elf fuel specification in Brazil, it naturally followed that Hill and Schumacher would also be faced with a problem in the event of their fuel being checked. Wisely, the Benetton and Williams team management kept

Despite leading the early stages at Monaco, he could not make sufficient ground on Schumacher's pursuing Benetton. Eventually he finished a bitterly disappointed second. Only later were problems with his car's differential blamed for the team selecting what proved to be the wrong race strategy (Darren Heath).

this controversy from the drivers, not wishing to unsettle them in the run-up to the race.

At the start, Schumacher went straight into the lead from second place on the grid and completed the opening lap 0.5sec ahead of Hill. Yet it certainly appeared that the German was under pressure and Damon seemed able to haul him in at will. By the time Schumacher headed for the pit lane for his first refuelling stop on lap 18, Hill had closed the gap to 0.2sec and after Michael lost time behind Rubens Barrichello's troubled Jordan at the pit entrance, Damon was able to capitalise on the situation and emerge ahead of the Benetton after his own first stop at the end of lap 21.

Once ahead, Hill began to ease confidently away. By lap 30 he was 3.4sec ahead of Schumacher — then things began to go wrong. 'I lost second gear coming out of one of the hairpins at the end of the lap,' he explained. 'Then going into the first turn at the start of lap 31, suddenly the rear end locked up and I just went off.' Although Damon may have initially suspected this was a transmission failure, in fact the pirouette was caused by a breakage in the left rear suspension.

That left Schumacher an easy run to victory from Coulthard, after which both were excluded — as expected — for the apparent fuel discrepancy. Both teams naturally appealed and the FIA international court of appeal duly reinstated them in the results, accepting that there were valid differences of opinion over whether or not the fuel discrepancy offered any performance benefit. Even so, Benetton and Williams were not allowed their Constructors' Championship points for first and second places.

The second round of the championship marked the return to Buenos Aires for the first Argentine GP to be staged since 1981. In the late 1970s, the race had invariably taken place in sweltering conditions at the end of January, but this later fixture in the first week of April guaranteed virtually endless rain throughout practice and qualifying.

Coulthard performed brilliantly, timing his fastest run to perfection with the assistance of the team management to take the first pole position of his career, Hill lining up second ahead of Schumacher.

Coulthard made a superb getaway to lead into the first corner, but in his wake a multiple collision was triggered by Alesi who forced his Ferrari down the still-wet inside line and then spun over the kerb, collecting several of his rivals. That caused the race to be red-flagged, but while Coulthard managed to repeat his perfect start second time round, Schumacher managed to split the Williams duo to take an early second place ahead of Hill.

Coulthard led for the first five laps before slowing suddenly with an electrical problem and dropping back to third. This left Michael leading from Damon and the Williams driver neatly outbraked his rival going into the first corner at the start of the 11th lap. Schumacher had found himself experiencing an unexpectedly premature deterioration in grip from his first set of tyres and was simply in no position to resist Hill's challenge, any more than he was from Coulthard who also slipped by into second place – round the outside of that first corner – five laps later.

From that point on, Hill felt confident that he could retain the upper hand and, although Schumacher regained the lead during the first spate of refuelling stops, Damon reasserted his advantage and won commandingly from Jean Alesi's Ferrari. Michael was third, but he underlined what was to come with a fastest race lap on his Benetton's fourth set of tyres which was 0.7sec quicker than Hill's best. Was this just a freak result? Or a definite signal of what was to follow later in the season?

The opening race of the European season was the San Marino GP at Imola, an emotional event for the entire F1 community marking, as it did, the first anniversary of Senna's fatal accident there. Damon only qualified fourth behind Schumacher, Gerhard Berger's Ferrari and Coulthard, but he demonstrated tremendous consistency and tactical skill to win the race after all his rivals encountered trouble in some form or another.

Damon left Imola leading the championship with 20 points, six ahead of Schumacher and Jean Alesi who tied for second place. It would be the only time all year that Hill headed the points table.

There were already problems in the pipeline for Hill and the Williams squad. Goodyear had made a front tyre construction change for Imola which Williams took some time to master. In addition, Benetton at last got to grips with the chassis set-up of its B195 in second qualifying at Barcelona – and Williams unexpectedly encountered a spate of hydraulic problems which would exact a high price on Damon's title hopes in terms of lost championship points.

Schumacher absolutely dominated the Spanish GP, yet it seemed as though Damon might survive with his points lead more or less intact. Running second after a three stop strategy, Hill went into his final lap confident that his six points for second place would allow him to keep ahead. Then the hydraulics failed.

'I went to select sixth gear, but it didn't happen,' explained Damon later. 'Something went wrong in the hydraulic system which runs the gearbox. At first it was OK, as it was stuck in fifth gear and you can

Inset *Absorbed in his thoughts. By Magny-Cours, Hill could sense that the 1995 World Championship might be slipping away from him (Darren Heath).*

Main picture *Lowest moment. Hill's Williams and Schumacher's Benetton beached in the gravel trap at Silverstone after their controversial collision as they battled for the lead of the 1995 British Grand Prix (Darren Heath).*

do a lap round here in fifth. But unfortunately the throttle system also works off the hydraulic pump.'

With only two downhill corners left to go, Hill's engine cut out and he was overtaken by Johnny Herbert's Benetton and Gerhard Berger's Ferrari as he coasted past the flag to take an eventual fourth. Damon acknowledged that Schumacher's season had picked up considerable momentum. 'We didn't have a good weekend,' he reflected. 'Our strategy was OK, but we just couldn't live with Michael's speed.' Schumacher now led the title chase with 24 points to Hill's 23.

Yet if Barcelona was a disappointment, it was as nothing compared with what was to follow at Monaco. Although Damon always played down the significance of the famous race through the streets of the

Damon qualified on pole at Hockenheim in front of Schumacher's home crowd, but delighted the German driver's supporters by spinning off while leading into the second lap of the race (ICN UK Bureau).

Principality, claiming it was of no more consequence than any other race on the calendar, such words lacked conviction. Winning on the circuit where his father triumphed five times was always going to be important, from the historic standpoint if nothing else.

Damon qualified magnificently on pole position, but then encountered trouble in the race morning warm-up. He could not better sixth fastest time in this half-hour session and was handicapped by a touch too much understeer. As Williams chief designer Adrian Newey subsequently explained, this was inadvertently responsible for leading the team down the wrong route as far as race strategy was concerned:

'Our lack of performance in the warm-up panicked us into deciding on a two stop refuelling strategy, because we thought everybody else would be going for two stops as well. The car was dreadful in the warm-up, so we concluded that it wasn't good on a half fuel load so perhaps it would be better in lighter trim. But the

trouble turned out to be a problem with the differential.'

Although Hill led from the start, Schumacher stayed close on his rear wing in the opening stages – even though the Benetton was only stopping once. Hill managed to pull out almost three seconds in the first 20 laps, but that time-consuming understeer in slow corners meant that he simply wasn't able to make any significant inroads into Michael's advantage once the Benetton was ahead. He finished the race second, in a deeply dejected mood, apparently unable to grasp how things had gone so horribly wrong for the team.

'I am bitterly disappointed not to have won here,' said Hill. 'The car was very good in qualifying and unfortunately didn't match up to that performance today. I knew it was going to be tough when I was not making any impression on Michael at the start. I knew then he had only one stop planned, yet I couldn't get away from him.'

Only when the Williams FW17 was stripped down on its return to the factory did the problem with the differential become clear. But that didn't alter the fact that Damon was now trailing Michael by five points as they headed for the Canadian GP in Montreal.

As far as Damon was concerned, the Canadian race was best forgotten as quickly as possible. Although he qualified alongside Schumacher on the front row of the grid, Hill found himself battling with poor chassis balance from the start, dropping as low as fourth place before eventually retiring with another hydraulic failure which first caused the car to jam in fifth gear and finally shut down the throttle control.

Despite gearchange trouble, Michael still managed to finish fifth to extend his points lead to seven on a day when Jean Alesi homed into a lucky maiden F1 victory at the wheel of his Ferrari. Hill, ever the realist, could already see his championship hopes coming apart.

The next three races saw Damon plunging headlong into what seemed increasingly like a nightmare without end. Not only were his ambitions heading straight for the rocks, but he increasingly found himself on the receiving end of Schumacher's waspish criticism as the German ace pressed home his on-track advantage with some well-aimed psychological attacks.

The first problem came after the French GP at Magny-Cours where Michael won easily after Damon lost crucial ground in traffic just prior to his first refuelling stop. On the face of it, the Williams race strategy still seemed to be lacking, but more serious were accusations from Schumacher that Hill had 'brake tested' his Benetton as they came up to lap one of the slow Forti-Fords early in the race.

Damon brushed aside the complaints. 'Michael is a great driver and

Right *Arms and the man. Damon before the start of the 1995 Hungarian GP where he checked Schumacher's rush towards the title with a well-judged win* (Darren Heath).

more than capable of looking after himself on the race track,' he replied firmly. 'I think he misjudged the manoeuvre in question and gave himself a bit of a fright. If he wants to talk to me about it, then I will be more than happy to do so.'

Yet the tension continued as Damon went into his home Grand Prix at Silverstone. Instead of arriving in a mood of surging optimism, Hill felt somewhat tense and preoccupied after the disappointments of the previous few races. It was also coming up to contract renewal time and striking the right deal looked as though it would be an increasingly difficult task for the Englishman as his title hopes hung in the balance. He now trailed Schumacher by 11 points (46 to 35) and the momentum had passed decisively to his rival.

Inevitably, plenty of muscle-flexing took place in the run-up to the British race. 'In my position,' said Hill, 'it's obvious that I am keen to talk to other teams, and that is what I have been doing. It's a little early to say anything further.' In fact, both Ferrari and Benetton had made tentative inquiries, although, ironically, both approaches were indirectly linked to Schumacher's plans.

I believe I'm a match for Michael as a driver, I intend to be a world champion

The bottom line was that Ferrari had taken the decision to bid for Schumacher. But if the German star was financially out of reach, Hill was an ideal alternative choice. In addition to his speed and proven track record was his talent as a test and development driver.

In much the same way, if Benetton *was* going to lose Schumacher to Ferrari, then Hill was the logical man for the job, particularly as he had plenty of experience with the Renault V10 engine. By the same token, Damon acknowledged that Schumacher was calling the shots in this particular market place.

'I'm obviously not going to earn more than Michael,' he admitted. 'He is the World Champion, which inevitably raises his value. He is currently playing the market and calling the shots, there is no mistaking that.

'But I certainly believe that I am a match for him as a driver and I intend to become a World Champion, so hopefully that will increase my value.'

Damon also hinted a belief that Frank Williams undervalues his drivers, perhaps to the detriment of their morale. In Hill's view, earning more money was not a goal in itself. 'But it is a measure of your value to a team,' he noted, effectively reiterating the message he had delivered in Adelaide the previous autumn. For a fleeting moment, some observers noted the sort of hard edge they once associated with Nigel Mansell. But it soon passed.

Of course, as far as Frank Williams was concerned, this was all water off a duck's back. Being supportive to his drivers when they were out of the cockpit had never been his line of country. Ever the 'cold father', he appeared profoundly unmoved by all the speculation and gossip, preferring the company of his engineers, technicians and — perhaps above all — his racing cars.

'I couldn't care less who Damon talks to,' he said. 'It's all perfectly healthy. I've probably talked to every driver in the pit lane 74 times this season.'

Yet there was worse to come in the race at Silverstone. Damon qualified on pole position and led commandingly in the opening phase of the race, buoyed up by the knowledge that Alesi's fast-starting Ferrari was keeping Schumacher back in third place. Yet Michael was only stopping once, Hill twice and he just failed to get back into the race after his own second stop at the end of lap 41 — with 20 left to run.

Coming into the braking area for the tight Priory left-hander on lap 46, Hill decided to go for it. He started his overtaking manoeuvre from slightly too far back and locked his left front wheel as he surged up inside the Benetton. Michael could have conceded the corner, but had no moral obligation to do so. He turned in — and the two cars

Don't crowd me. Schumacher and Hill wheel-to-wheel for the lead of the 1995 Belgian GP at Spa. Damon gave Michael a piece of his mind as far as driving etiquette was concerned once this confrontation was over (ICN UK Bureau).

collided, spinning into retirement in the gravel trap on the outside of the corner.

While Damon attempted to explain away the episode as nothing more than a racing accident, Schumacher used the opportunity to lambast Hill yet again in public.

'What Damon did there was completely unnecessary,' he claimed. 'There was no room and he came from nowhere. I just don't see the sense of doing things like this, even in front of your home crowd. You have to keep your nerve and temperament and not be a danger to anyone.

'It's more or less the same situation as Adelaide where he tried to dive inside and there was no room. I can't understand it. Damon was probably under too much pressure and tried to do something that wouldn't work.'

Many people regarded Schumacher's comparison of the Silverstone and Adelaide incidents as somewhat cheeky. A strong body of F1 opinion maintained that he had been the sole architect of the previous year's Australian GP shunt.

Damon could at least console himself with some pleasure on the family front in the week after the Silverstone race when his wife Georgie gave birth to a daughter, Tabitha, their third child following on after two boys.

Yet reports in the British daily press that Frank Williams had labelled Damon 'a prat' did little to soothe his spirits. It had been suggested that Williams made this crack when he dropped by the Benetton garage at the end of the race, possibly to apologise to Flavio Briatore and Schumacher.

These reports surfaced on a day when an official press statement from Williams was issued endorsing Hill's driving. It read: 'Both Frank and Patrick (Head) are very supportive of Damon. They appreciate the way he played the incident down, just like we did after Adelaide last year. This is motor racing, this sort of thing happens. Damon is the man chosen to drive the race. If he feels he had to go for it, then we back his decision.'

This was followed speedily by a personal statement from Frank Williams claiming that reports that he labelled Damon a prat and apologised to Benetton were 'totally erroneous'.

Experienced F1 watchers found it difficult to separate fact from fiction. Although Williams put on this public show of support for its number one driver, there was little doubt that the episode could have seriously damaged Hill's bargaining position. Yet on the Tuesday after the race, Hill was still saying 'I felt there was a genuine chance to attack him as he had taken a wide line. I believe that, and I don't think I did anything wrong'.

In fairness, it has to be said that many people agreed with that

Accelerating out onto the Monza circuit prior to the start of the 1995 Italian GP. Damon's collision with Schumacher made this another race to forget (Darren Heath).

viewpoint. Perhaps Schumacher did indeed take a wide line, intending to tempt Hill into over-braking and sliding straight across his bows into the gravel trap? Others felt that Schumacher was simply determined not to allow Hill the satisfaction of winning on home ground – at any cost.

Interestingly, once they had examined the video evidence, the stewards of the meeting issued a severe reprimand to both drivers. It was clear that they regarded Schumacher as at least partly to blame.

For Hill, the delight over the birth of his daughter would be followed by another helping of professional disappointment in the German Grand Prix at Hockenheim. Crowning a weekend marked by the worst xenophobic excesses on the part of an unpleasant minority of fans wearing 'Kill Hill' tee shirts, Damon again played straight into Schumacher's hands by spinning off the road into a gravel trap at the first corner after the pits while leading into the second lap.

Schumacher got stuck into him again: 'For sure, Damon made a big mistake. He should have known that there would be some deposits on the track at this point. I knew that it would be slippery, because everybody drops some oil on the first lap, so I braked early.

Tucking in tightly behind team-mate David Coulthard's Williams at the start of the 1995 Portuguese GP while Ukyo Katayama's Tyrrell prompts the red flag as it collides with a Minardi in the background. At the restart, Hill got away slowly and Schumacher nipped in ahead of him (ICN UK Bureau).

'Then I saw Damon suddenly go sideways and thought "I can't believe this". Then he hit the wall, and I thought "Fine, that's it."' Michael was thus left to cruise to an easy victory.

Perhaps seeking to mollify Hill at a crucial moment in the season, Williams put out a sympathetic statement. 'We have identified a left-hand rear driveshaft joint showing signs of unusual wear,' said Patrick Head. 'It is not beyond reasonable doubt that this could well have contributed to the spin.' Others within the Williams camp thought this was being over-generous, almost to a fault. But they kept such thoughts to themselves.

Damon regained his composure by scoring a decisive victory in the Hungarian GP where the Williams FW17's high downforce configuration exacted a performance advantage over the Benetton on the tight Hungaroring circuit, but Schumacher failed to finish this race anyway.

'This was the best win of my F1 career,' said Hill jubilantly. 'It was a race I had to win, and I won it, so it was a bit of a pay-back day for me. I think we were pretty well in control throughout. Everything went to plan. It was not really clear, but after Schumacher's last stop, we needed a clean stop to get out ahead of him again. But traffic was a problem and it was not over until he dropped out. I was mightily relieved, but I think we had him beaten.'

Michael now had 56 points in the championship table with Hill slashing his advantage from 21 to 11. It was a timely boost for the Englishman's fortunes, to be followed a few days later by an announcement that he had concluded a contract for the 1996 season, reputedly in the order of £5 million. At the same time, it was confirmed that Coulthard's place as Damon's team-mate would be taken by Indycar star Jacques Villeneuve, son of the legendary Ferrari driver Gilles who had keen killed practising for the 1982 Belgian Grand Prix.

For the moment, Hill had a smile on his face: 'I think any time you can have a choice of teams that are at the top, you have to consider yourself to be in a very privileged position'. Was he being enigmatic? Was the tide changing? Or was that victory at Budapest only a momentary blip in Michael Schumacher's relentless march towards another World Championship?

European GP, Nurburgring. Making a race of it with Schumacher's Benetton. Michael won, Damon spun out. The World Championship had all-but slipped from his grasp (Darren Heath).

Heavy traffic. Muscling into the first turn of the 1995 Pacific GP, Hill points his Williams tight onto Coulthard's tail as he slices inside Schumacher. But Michael won from David, with Damon trailing home third. The title battle was now over (ICN UK Bureau).

In fact, it turned out to be the latter. From that point onwards, the Englishman was definitely on the run.

Hill came out of the Belgian Grand Prix with second place, his chances finally dashed by the need to return to the pit for a 10sec stop-go penalty for exceeding the pit lane speed limit. That dropped him to third behind Martin Brundle's Ligier, but he demolished Brundle's advantage with a succession of blistering laps and just managed to squeeze past into second place mid-way round the final lap.

In the aftermath of the Belgian GP, where Schumacher scored one of his best victories over Damon, driving up through the field from 16th place on the grid, the German received a one race ban suspended for four races after banging wheels with Hill.

Damon issued a brisk, if slightly oblique, critique of Schumacher's driving tactics, making it clear that he felt his rival had blatantly blocked him at a point where his Williams had a performance advantage on wet weather tyres on the still-damp track.

'If the rules do not prevent drivers from using cars as instruments to prevent other drivers from overtaking – in other words to forcibly drive at another car – then the rules are wrong, aren't they?' he queried.

96

'If the rules say we can go out there and smash into each other as much as we want, then I'll make a decision as to whether or not I want to be in this sport.

'I have told Michael what I thought of his driving, but anyone who comes through from 16th place on the grid to win deserves to be congratulated. But I could have won, but for a bit of bad luck. The conditions were very tricky and Michael drove a stupendous race. I'm just sorry I wasn't able to be there at the end to give him some competition.

'We had some pretty hairy moments, and I must say that I am not satisfied with being driven into. Michael drove very defensively, to the point of touching wheels with me at the top of the hill.

'That's all well and good if it's accidental, but if it's meant on purpose, I would be pretty upset. These are F1 cars, not go-karts. Some things are acceptable, some are not, and Michael will have his own view about it, I expect.'

For once it seemed as though Damon had got Schumacher squirming slightly with embarrassment. Perhaps relieved at the subtlety with which Hill had delivered the thinly veiled rebuke, he agreed with the

Williams 1–2 at the start of the 1995 Australian GP, the last such race to be held at Adelaide (ICN UK Bureau).

sentiments in an over-anxious, Little Boy Lost fashion. 'I think that is absolutely right,' he said. 'Touching wheels in high speed corners is not acceptable, but at the speed we were doing, I think you can do this. We are professional drivers and know how to keep these cars on the road.'

Then came the pain and disappointment at Monza where Hill retired after running into the back of Schumacher, and his season degenerated into chaos. Third in Portugal behind Coulthard's winning Williams and Schumacher was followed up by spinning off at Nurburgring after an earlier collision with Alesi's Ferrari. That gave Michael even more ammunition with which to undermine his rival.

Prior to the Pacific GP at Aida, the race in which Michael clinched his second world title, he commented: 'Damon's biggest problem is that he doesn't appear to be in control when he is trying to overtake. He makes half-hearted attempts which land him in trouble, with no way out.'

He looked like a man who had come through the eye of a storm — and survived

At least Hill got some measure of consolation in the race, where he adopted some extremely defensive tactics early on. Schumacher complained bitterly, but Damon — who had earlier sought advice from the FIA as to what was acceptable and what was not — came straight out and told Michael that his objections were completely extraordinary.

'The situation now is that we are completely free to drive as we like as long as it is not deliberately dangerous,' he grinned. 'So I drove in that style and he did not like it. But he should have no complaints; it seems that there is one rule for him and another for everybody else.'

Third place in the Pacific GP was a disappointment for Damon, but worse was to come when he spun into a gravel trap during the following weekend's Japanese GP at Suzuka. It was one of those moments when one could almost detect the Williams team losing its faith in him — again.

In an effort to forestall such assumptions, Frank Williams offered a firmly upbeat endorsement of his driver. 'If he's getting a slagging off (in the press) that must mean he is as good as Nigel Mansell used to be, he must have attained Nigel's eminence,' said Frank, not altogether convincingly.

'You say he has taken a bit of a pounding? Before Aida, I read for the second time a marvellous book about Wellington and Waterloo. He said "by God, we are taking a pounding". But let's see who can pound the hardest. Do you see what I mean?

'I have had doubts about him, of course; you cannot ignore your problems, and he had obviously gone off the boil a couple of times.

Back on the rails again. The Williams crew celebrates Damon's fourth win of the 1995 title chase as the season ends in the Adelaide pit lane (Darren Heath).

But he is improving all the time. We have made our decision and are happy with it.'

Damon simply remarked 'I understand more about the pressures involved in trying to win a championship than I did last year'. For the cynical, these remarks seemed just a little too glib – as if the Williams team had decided that all the partners in this disappointing season should be seen to be saying the right things before slinking off to lick their wounds.

Hill's departure from the Japanese race came when he was running in fourth place. But he was also fined $10,000 for exceeding the pit lane speed limit.

Immediately after the race, he cleared off on holiday to Bali with

Georgie, had a good think about everything, and returned for the final race of the season in a completely revitalised frame of mind. Frank Williams later confessed that he was extremely impressed over the way in which Damon had changed: 'Whatever he did, he did completely on his own'.

In purely historical terms, one could say that Damon Hill's decisive transformation in preparation for 1996 began with the Australian GP the previous November. He drove with dogged determination to win after team-mate Coulthard collided with the pit wall as he came in for his first refuelling stop.

It was a curious race of changing fortunes. Virtually all the front runners retired, leaving Damon with the task of consolidating a massive advantage which would be stretched at the end to two laps over Olivier Panis's Ligier-Mugen.

It was a little like the 1993 Budapest GP all over again. Hill could only lose the race. There was a nail-biting moment in the closing stages when a front left-wheel nut cross-threaded itself at the final refuelling stop and the Williams was stationary for an agonising 22.1sec. Had anyone been closer, his advantage would have been in serious jeopardy.

At the end of the race, Damon radiated the demeanour of a man who had come through the eye of the storm. And survived. The Australian Grand Prix victory had been, more than anything else, a symbolic reaffirmation of his own self-confidence. It would serve as a springboard for 1996 and enabled him to go into the off-season basking in the afterglow of success rather than the failure which had gone before.

Yet as Hill jetted back to Europe, he had other things on his mind as well. Not only would the 1996 season represent a moment of truth for him personally, but the fact that David Coulthard was leaving to join McLaren to be replaced at Williams by the much-heralded Indycar champion Jacques Villeneuve meant that Hill was going to be faced with a potent challenge from his own team-mate, as well as the usual threats from the rest of the field. There would certainly be some close racing ahead.

Challenging for the Championship

4

'As I walked back to the de-briefing room after the Suzuka race, I hadn't known whether to laugh or cry. If I hadn't laughed, I would have certainly cried. So there was no choice but to laugh.' With those words, Damon Hill summed up his catastrophic outing in the 1995 Japanese Grand Prix.

This was the lowest point in his F1 career. A fortnight later, as Frank Williams has recounted, he emerged from the doldrums a different man and won a psychologically demanding, if tactically straightforward Australian GP at Adelaide.

It was the last such race to be held through the streets of the South Australia state capital. For 1996, the race would switch to Melbourne's freshly revamped Albert Park circuit, 30 years after Stirling Moss won there in Australia's Olympic year.

From a wider perspective, it has to be said that the tone for Damon Hill's 1996 season was established in that final race of the previous season. He was more focused, somehow calmer, than he had been at any moment in the 1995 season. And he would return to Australia three months later with the steely confidence of a man who realised that he had no place left to hide.

In 1996 the 35-year old British driver fully appreciated that he had to win the World Championship. He was shrewd enough to judge that it might be now or never; that his failure to deliver the goods might just make it difficult to retain his place in the F1 front rank for 1997. Having twice finished second to Michael Schumacher, in 1994 and 1995, now he had everything going for him: added maturity, experience, sheer racing nous – and in a season when all the top drivers except himself had moved to new teams, he had familiarity with the car, the boss and the crew. As one paddock sage put it, 'they know how he likes his tea'.

By the same token of course, he had more than most to lose.

Yet there was one decisive factor in his favour that had been absent before. Hill started the season armed with the most competitive, mechanically proven car. Moreover, he would be hoping that Schumacher's new position at the wheel of an all-new and unproven Ferrari would leave him a clear run down the fast lane to the championship crown.

Hill was sufficiently seasoned to appreciate that the Formula 1 business was considerably more complex than that. He squared up to several other key rivals, not least his new team-mate, 1995 Indycar Champion Jacques Villeneuve, who might be new to Formula 1 but was being hailed in Britain as the hottest thing since Senna, a driver who could *really* give Schumacher a run for his money.

Hill remained firm in his personal belief that he was better prepared than ever before to deliver a consistent string of strong performances.

'I think the wins will be spread around more this season,' he predicted. 'There are too many good drivers in good cars for anybody to have a decisive, clear-cut advantage. For myself, my motivation is high, but I feel more relaxed about the challenge ahead of me. Being more relaxed I hope will enable me to perform better.

'I suppose you could describe it as the "been there, done it" factor. I feel a bit more comfortable about the future; perhaps another year's experience will help me to better recognise situations as they develop. But I will certainly be out there to win races and, ultimately, the championship.'

Despite this, Hill still found it a little surprising that he was regarded as pre-season favourite: 'If I am favourite, I take that as a compliment, but I wouldn't say it would be by a big margin. I think the competition will be close, I think that the season will be more complex than simply thinking in terms of Jean Alesi's Benetton or Michael's Ferrari, for example.

'As far as Jacques is concerned, he obviously still has a lot to learn about F1, but he is clearly very quick. He is Indycar Champion, winner of the Indy 500, and is certainly intending to make his mark. So there will be challenges from all directions this season.'

Yet going into his fourth F1 season with Williams, Damon remained something of an enigma to many in the motor racing community, including some members of his own team. This is largely down to the fact that his graduation to F1 did not follow a period of sustained success in the junior formulae.

There was also the need to exorcise the ghosts of 1995, a season which saw him make too many errors of judgement, including those two highly publicised collisions with Schumacher's Benetton at Silverstone and Monza. He vowed to be more consistent, avoiding the downward lurches in form which sluiced away his championship chances in the second half of the last season.

On a treacherously slippery track surface, Hill's 1996 Brazilian GP triumph underlined the message of Suzuka 16 months earlier — Damon is a fine wet weather driver . . . (Darren Heath)

. . . A tactically shrewd late refuelling stop helped too (ICN UK Bureau).

Physical fitness was a key element in Hill's armoury. He was now training sometimes up to six hours a day and had installed his own gymnasium at home. He had forced the pace of his physical preparation for the 1996 season to fresh levels of excellence. Mentally and physically he believed he had never been better geared up to take on the championship challenge.

The equipment at Hill's gym included a system of weights which could be attached to his helmet in order to simulate the lateral G-forces experienced at various circuits on the calendar.

He would later recall that this was of particular benefit in preparing for the Brazilian GP. Sao Paulo's Interlagos circuit is one of the few on the schedule to run in an anti-clockwise direction. With that in mind, strengthening the neck muscles would take on a particular importance – although as it happened, on race day it rained hard and the driving was nowhere near as physically demanding as Damon had anticipated due to the wet track and slower lap times.

The disciplined approach to this physical regime was prompted by fitness instructor Erwin Gollner who was signed by the Williams team in 1995. During the winter Damon submitted himself to a training 'holiday' with Gollner in the Austrian mountains.

After being put through a gruelling series of tests 'on all sorts of weird machines', including one designed to test reactions, Hill was gratified to learn that, out of thousands of other athletes who had tried this particular machine, he had come out ahead of them all.

'Quite honestly, I would like to be fitter than I am now when I am 45,' mused Damon later in the season. 'And I think that is possible. I'm pretty committed to physical fitness and training, so I certainly believe that I can keep myself in trim. After all, Fangio was 48, or whatever, when he stopped, so I don't think I have to worry about my future much at the age of 36!'

Come the opening race in Melbourne, Damon Hill started where he left off the previous November by dodging through to score a fortunate victory at the splendid new Albert Park circuit. Yet he only took the lead with four of the race's 58 laps left to run when his dynamic new team-mate Jacques Villeneuve was forced to concede almost certain victory when he slowed with fading oil pressure less than 20 miles from the chequered flag.

'The car ran perfectly the whole way through,' said Hill after the race. 'My only problem was that I somehow got a stone down my back with about 30 laps to go and I was shifting about in the seat trying to move it. Every time I moved, it slipped to somewhere else even less comfortable.'

While the motor racing fraternity rightly feted Villeneuve for a superb effort on his grand prix debut, the fact remained that Hill had shown great restraint and assurance in what for him was a ticklish situation. Had he settled for second, he would have been accused of dragging his feet; if he had become over-anxious and collided with Villeneuve, he would have risked the disapproval of his team. Under the circumstances, he did just right, keeping his cool and accelerating cleanly through to win when Villeneuve's dramatic challenge was spent.

From the outset the two Williams-Renaults had seldom been more than a second apart at the head of the field, with Villeneuve starting from pole and beating Hill convincingly on the sprint to the first corner on the opening lap. In fact, Damon's race almost ended as he swung into that first turn. His Williams snapped sideways with the result that he lost momentum and was overhauled by the Ferraris of Michael Schumacher and Eddie Irvine as they accelerated down the following straight.

In tactical terms, this was a potential disaster for Hill. Villeneuve was already easing away in the distance and, with the two Williamses scheduled to make a single refuelling stop, the Englishman was now in a position of being boxed in behind two Ferraris which were benefiting from their lighter fuel load in the early stages of the race.

'I made a complete pig's ear of the first start,' Damon admitted. 'I

Controlling the pressure. Hill keeps ahead of Michael Schumacher's Ferrari F310 and the Benetton B196 of Jean Alesi in the opening phase of the 1996 Argentine Grand Prix (Darren Heath).

The spoils of victory. Georgie Hill congratulates her man after his third win of the 1996 season in Buenos Aires (Darren Heath).

got very sideways and thought this is going to be a long old race stuck behind these two Ferraris.'

In the event, Hill got a second chance when the race was restarted following Martin Brundle's first lap accident, and didn't make the same mistake again. He ran second from the outset and even squeezed ahead of Villeneuve as he rejoined the race following his refuelling stop. But the French-Canadian immediately repassed him in audacious fashion and stayed ahead before suffering mechanical trouble.

'I can't describe what it feels like,' said Damon, savouring his victory. 'It is a long time since I was leading the World Championship and obviously I feel on top of the world. It was terrific, I had a great race with Jacques and I am delighted to have come back to Australia and won. I have started the season where I finished the last one.'

As an afterthought, Damon pointed out that every year since 1990, the driver who had won the first race of the season had gone on to win the World Championship. 'I don't intend to break with that tradition,' he said bullishly.

On the rostrum it was Hill's chance to look elated — and Michael's to be dejected

Three weeks later, Hill would deliver more of the same in Brazil. At Sao Paulo's bumpy, punishing Interlagos track, he produced a flawless drive in precarious and unpredictably changing weather conditions to win the second round of the title chase. It was as decisive a success as his opening win in Melbourne had been fortuitous.

This was Hill's 15th win, beating his father Graham's total of 14, and left him heading the title chase with 20 points, 14 ahead of Jean Alesi whose Benetton finished second some 20.6sec behind, the Frenchman tying on points with Villeneuve. The Canadian new boy had ended his second grand prix by spinning into a gravel trap while battling with Alesi for second place.

Having qualified on pole position almost a second faster than Rubens Barrichello's Jordan-Peugeot, Hill found all his pre-race calculations thrown into disarray when a torrential downpour doused the circuit only 40 minutes before the start. Yet despite this unpredictable lottery, Hill led from start to finish and never put a wheel out of line.

At the start Hill moved neatly across to protect his advantage from Barrichello as they made for the first corner, allowing Villeneuve to aim the other Williams FW18 round the outside in an effort to nose ahead in the scrum.

Jacques pulled level on the outside and the two team-mates were wheel-to-wheel as they braked for the first right hander, but with Damon on the inside line he was able to assert his advantage as they streamed away down the first long straight.

By the end of the opening lap Hill came slamming across the

Not so tidy. Having qualified on pole position for the 1996 European GP, Damon made a shocking getaway and immediately dropped back to fifth place. Here Jacques Villeneuve takes a winning advantage at the first corner pursued by David Coulthard's McLaren, Rubens Barrichello's Jordan and Hill bumping the kerb as he battles alongside Schumacher's Ferrari (ICN UK Bureau).

start/finish line already a couple of seconds ahead of Villeneuve with Alesi, Barrichello, Schumacher, Martin Brundle's Jordan and the thrusting Jos Verstappen's Footwork-Hart all behind. Hill was six seconds ahead on his second lap after a spurt which decisively stamped his authority on proceedings from the outset. From then on, it was just a question of seeing which of his rivals would finish second.

When the track began to dry out in parts, Alesi cut into Hill's advantage, reducing his lead from 17.5sec on lap 29 to 13.1sec only two laps later. Then Alesi made a slight mistake and dropped back behind Barrichello, being promoted again to second when the Brazilian came in for his sole refuelling stop at the end of lap 34.

Tyre strategy now looked set to play a crucial part in the outcome of the race. Hill had sufficient fuel in his Williams to stay out until the end of lap 40 of this 71 lap race, taking the opportunity to switch to dry weather slicks at his sole stop. With the track still treacherously slippery in places this certainly looked like a high risk gamble, but Damon vindicated the decision by immediately knocking seven seconds off the previous fastest race lap on his return to the circuit.

In the closing stages of the race, Hill lapped Schumacher's third place Ferrari. It was a delicious moment for Damon, but he didn't crow about it. Although looking very browned off Michael made some complimentary remarks about Damon's performance at the post race press conference.

On the rostrum this was the supreme role reversal. Here it was Damon's chance to look elated – and Schumacher's turn to look dejected and self-absorbed. It was all very different from 1994 and 1995.

Hill received an added bonus in the form of a very public endorsement from Louis Schweitzer, the chairman of Renault who was visiting Brazil to lay the foundations for a new car factory. Engine suppliers to Williams since 1989, Renault were confidently anticipating that Hill's efforts would deliver the French car maker their fourth constructors' title in five seasons.

'I was very impressed with Damon Hill who dominated the race from beginning to end with a skilful and wise drive,' said the Renault chief. 'He showed today he has the qualities to be a World Champion.'

Four days later, Damon arrived in the paddock at Buenos Aires in preparation for the third round.

'In case you were wondering, I went to Rio after Sao Paulo,' he said. 'I had a nice time there for three days. Those three days seemed like a long time; I packed a lot in, had a good time. Played tennis, played golf, went wind surfing and enjoyed myself basically, with a view to coming here and enjoying myself even more, if I can. And there's no reason why that can't be the case.

'I didn't spend too long thinking about motor racing, but now I'm here my mind is on the job.'

The Buenos Aires circuit represented a totally different challenge from Interlagos. Damon likened it to the Hungaroring circuit near Budapest, venue for the Hungarian GP, the race which had marked his first F1 success back in 1993. Fairly smooth, with little in the way of elevation changes, the Autodromo Oscar Galvez is a high downforce track with plenty of tight radius corners with bumpy braking areas.

For all that, Hill remained confident. 'I don't see any reason why anything should have changed here,' he predicted. 'I think the competition will be close, but I think the circuit could suit more cars than Interlagos, perhaps. Here it is not so demanding on the chassis. Myself, I feel fine and great.'

His predictions were right on the button. Starting from pole position, he moved on to match Stirling Moss's tally of 16 victories with a technically straightforward, yet psychologically challenging win. Despite an upset stomach and the fact that an inoperative radio left him isolated from his crew on the pit wall, Hill kept control ahead of Schumacher's Ferrari by the smallest of margins in the opening stages before pulling away commandingly.

'It doesn't get any better than this,' he grinned, after crossing the line 12.1s ahead of his team-mate Jacques Villeneuve. 'The car ran perfectly and the only problem I had was the lack of radio communication throughout. Also I haven't been able to keep anything down for the past few days and I was worried about my physical stamina.'

The victory came despite three frustrating laps behind the safety car after Luca Badoer contrived to upend his ponderous Forti after sliding off the circuit on lap 25. Four laps later Pedro Diniz's Ligier apparently exploded in a ball of flame out on the circuit after a problem during his refuelling stop.

A return valve in the Ligier's car-mounted refuelling nozzle stuck open and, as he braked hard for a tight infield right-hander, fuel began to spew from the orifice all over the car's exhaust system. The fire raged for over 20sec during which time Diniz speedily removed himself from the scene. This excitement allowed Schumacher to tuck in behind his Williams rival in a slow moving queue after the safety car was deployed to hold back the pack. But after the Renault Clio pulled off into the pit lane, Hill quickly reasserted his advantage and eased open his lead.

Schumacher, having long since calculated the only way his Ferrari F310 could compete with Hill's pole-winning Williams was by planning a three stop strategy, kept within striking distance of Damon in the opening stages before gradually dropping back into the clutches of Jean Alesi's much-improved Benetton B196.

Shortly before making his first refuelling stop at the end of lap 21, Schumacher's car had been hit by some debris apparently thrown up by Hill's rear wheel. The unidentified flying object hit the rear wing, causing the rear flap gradually to loosen itself, much to the detriment of the Ferrari's handling. Eventually Michael would retire.

Alesi ran strongly and looked as though he might be in with a shout for Benetton. But on lap 40, he stalled at his second refuelling stop and lost all chance of success. Berger picked up the Benetton standard before sliding off the track with a broken rear torsion bar while running second with 15 laps to go.

Jacques Villeneuve – who'd been badly boxed in after a slow start and was grappling with clutch slip in the closing stages – surged through to complete a Williams 1–2.

Alesi wound up third ahead of Barrichello, the only finisher to run one stop after taking advice from Goodyear that the Jordan 196 would go the distance on a single change of rubber.

It had been a glorious day for Damon. He had now won the first three races of the season under widely contrasting circumstances during

Right *Lost in thought – and determined not to allow anybody else into the World Championship lead* (Darren Heath).

which he demonstrated great versatility and control. However, over toasted sandwiches in the bar at Buenos Aires's Ezeiza airport later that same evening, Benetton boss Flavio Briatore confidently bet the author £500 that Jean Alesi would pick up the threads of his season and end up beating Hill to the World Championship.

'Jean has become very disciplined since he joined us at Benetton,' said Briatore. 'He has the speed necessary to win the championship and with some new technical developments in the pipeline I think we will soon be in a position to beat the Williams. Gerhard Berger is also very competitive in our car, as he showed at Buenos Aires where he was also running second in the closing stages.'

On the strength of what we'd seen so far in 1996, this seemed a decidedly optimistic forecast, so it was with a light heart that the writer downed his beer and accepted the bet with a degree of relish before we all climbed aboard the British Airways Boeing 747-400 for the non-stop flight back to Heathrow in the custody and control of Captain Kenneth Tyrrell, elder son of F1 team chief Ken Tyrrell. Money didn't look likely to come much easier than that.

The Williams-Renault team's domination of the 1996 World Championship would be sustained through the opening two races of the European season. Jacques Villeneuve scored a commanding win in the European GP in only his fourth ever F1 race – matching the achievement of Emerson Fittipaldi at Watkins Glen in 1970 – while Damon, fourth at Nurburgring, reasserted himself at the top of the victory podium at Imola a week later with a brilliantly judged success in the San Marino GP on the second anniversary of Ayrton Senna's death.

Yet Frank Williams and his crew were alert to possible challenges from several other areas. In particular, the performance of both Michael Schumacher and the McLaren-Mercedes team in these two races suggested that Hill's march towards the World Championship was certainly far from a guaranteed result.

If anything, the first two European races emphasised his need to pack away the points as quickly as possible before these rivals developed their equipment to a winning pitch.

Specifically, anyone doubting Schumacher's driving genius – and wanting to see precisely what Ferrari was getting for its reputed $20 million annual investment – only had to watch the German ace as he battled through the hour-long qualifying session before his home crowd at Nurburgring.

When it came to sheer grip, the Ferrari just wasn't in the same class as Damon's Williams. The Englishman could place his car within inches of a chosen spot anywhere round the circuit. His precision was a joy to behold. But in Michael's case, it was different. The Ferrari was like a wayward stallion and Schumacher was having to rein it in with all the car control he could muster.

Generous in defeat. Having finished fourth in the 1996 European GP, Damon steps forward to congratulate team-mate Jacques Villeneuve who has just notched up his first Formula 1 victory (Darren Heath).

Williams team fitness guru Erwin Gollner. Damon attributes much of his fitness to the Austrian's highly disciplined training regime (Darren Heath).

Hill with Adrian Newey, the architect behind the best car on the 1996 F1 starting grid (ICN UK Bureau).

Yet Schumacher remained enormously upbeat about the Italian team's long term chances. 'With the developments we currently have in the pipeline, I would expect that we would be in a position to start challenging for victory by the French GP,' he said brightly.

'As far as this race here at Nurburgring is concerned, if I am on the podium then that is a success. But the Williams is out of reach, for the moment at least. We have to accept that, although Ferrari is doing a great job, it will be mid-season before we are winning and that will be too late for the World Championship.'

Hanging on in there. Damon's Williams FW18 heads Michael Schumacher's Ferrari just after the Englishman rejoined the 1996 San Marino GP following his second refuelling stop (Darren Heath).

However, it was a credit to Villeneuve's resilience under pressure that he simply wasn't about to be intimidated by Schumacher's presence in his mirrors. Ferrari President Luca di Montezemolo may have ventured the suggestion that, had it not been for Coulthard staying ahead of Schumacher before making his second refuelling stop at the end of lap 46, things might have been different. But, interestingly, Schumacher made no reference to this apparent incident and reckoned that Coulthard had driven extremely well.

For his part, Damon had a troubled afternoon after a poor start from pole position and could count himself fortunate to finish fourth, having slipped as low as 11th at one point during the race's early stages.

Deeply concerned about an apparently strange handling imbalance on

his first set of tyres, Damon radioed to his pit that he thought he had a puncture or a rear suspension problem. The team brought him in for his first refuelling stop three laps ahead of schedule, after surviving a lurid brush with Pedro Diniz's Ligier as he squeezed past the Brazilian to take ninth place.

In the closing stages, Hill got well into his stride again but just failed to catch his former team-mate David Coulthard who scored the first podium finish of the season for the McLaren-Mercedes after a fine drive which did much for his confidence. 'I wanted to finish third, but then so did David,' shrugged Hill afterwards.

Coulthard said he had not been intimidated by Hill's presence in his mirrors in the closing stages of the race. Knowing how Damon operates Coulthard shrewdly judged that he would not force the issue. 'I blocked him a bit,' said the Scot. 'I knew he would settle for the points under these circumstances and not take any risks.'

A week later at Imola, Schumacher took his first Ferrari pole in brilliant fashion, edging out Hill's Williams with three minutes of qualifying left to run, but then spun off at the Tamburello chicane only seconds after posting the time. The F310 had suffered a failure of its left rear suspension and the team's mechanics were forced to work all night to rectify the problem in a manner which would hopefully prevent a repeat performance on race day.

It was the intervention of David Coulthard's much improved McLaren-Mercedes which in some small measure contributed to Schumacher's frustration in the early stages of the race. Michael had clearly expected to accelerate cleanly into the lead going into the first corner, but he made an uncharacteristically slow start and was passed by both Coulthard and Hill going down to the first chicane.

At the end of the opening lap, Schumacher sliced past Hill to take second place, but at this point Damon knew precisely what he was doing. He knew that Coulthard would hold up the Ferrari slightly and that Williams were set to beat the field on their race strategy alone.

When Schumacher and Coulthard made their first stops, Damon surged past and did not stop until he had completed lap 30. This convinced some observers that the Williams might only be stopping once, but Hill's car took on little more than 70-litres at the first refuelling stop.

Williams had done some astute calculations as regards fuel

Inset *Celebrating together. Hill looks satisfied with his fourth win out of five races, while Schumacher clearly reckons second place from pole position in the new Ferrari F310 is as much as he could have expected at Imola. Berger is glad to be there on the podium too (Darren Heath).*

Main picture *Brilliant start. On a slippery track surface, Damon accelerates into an immediate lead from second place on the grid at the 1996 Monaco GP . . . (ICN UK Bureau).*

. . . But had a bitterly disappointing finish. Abandoning his Williams FW18 in the chicane escape road after being denied a superb victory due to oil pump failure (Darren Heath).

Contemplating the relentless downpour on the morning of the 1996 Spanish GP (Darren Heath).

Damon would like his fans to have the last word (ICN UK Bureau).

consumption in the race. They had reasoned that Damon would not begin lapping slower cars until around lap 24, after which he would be in traffic for much of the race. It thus made most sense to run the second half of the race with two shorter stints – one of 20 laps, the other of 11 – to keep the car as agile and responsive as possible when he needed to pick a path through the backmarkers.

Damon admits that he went to the grid harbouring some reservations in the back of his mind and was asking for reassurance that the strategy would work almost to the moment he set off on his final parade lap. But chief designer Adrian Newey and his engineers were confident that their calculations were correct and Damon, ever the team player, accepted their well-reasoned assurances.

As events unfolded, the strategy was not a problem. In the second half of the race he was comfortably ahead of the opposition, the key moment in consolidating his position coming when he got out from his first stop 0.9sec ahead of Schumacher. Damon had no need to hurry at this point, knowing full well that all he had to do was keep calm and not allow himself to be ruffled.

The engine failure was a bitter blow for Damon and a taste of things to come

That said, there were moments when Hill had things lucky. By lap 46, Schumacher found himself boxed in behind an undisciplined battle for tenth place between Mika Hakkinen's McLaren and Pedro Diniz in the Ligier. Over the course of a couple of laps, Michael lost four seconds before the warring duo were quite rightly called into the pits for 10sec stop-go penalties as their reward for ignoring the waved blue warning flags.

Hill eventually took the chequered flag 16.4sec ahead of Schumacher, with Gerhard Berger third and Eddie Irvine fourth in the second Ferrari. Damon had now won four out of the first five races of the season. He had 43 points to Villeneuve's 22. Things were looking good.

Then came Monaco. For Hill and Williams it was the race which would be remembered throughout the season as very definitely The One Which Got Away.

Michael Schumacher stormed to pole position after a brilliant qualifying effort had seen his F310 edge out the optimistic Damon Hill by a whisker. Heavy rain before the start had eased, all but one of the pack was still on rain tyres as they sprinted for the tricky Ste Devote right-hander, and Damon stormed up the outside to take a decisive lead. What came next was simply unbelievable. Mid-way round the opening lap Michael Schumacher lost it. The Champ just slid wide on the right-hander before Portier and took his left front wheel off against the guard rail. Just like Ayrton Senna had done back in 1988 a few yards further on.

Sportsmen all. Damon takes advice from triple World Champion Niki Lauda (ICN UK Bureau).

Can Frenchman and Newcastle United striker David Ginola offer any advice (ICN UK Bureau)

Nick Faldo joins Damon at the 1996 British GP. Hill regards the golfing legend as one of his greatest sporting heroes (ICN UK Bureau).

That left Damon with the race in his pocket. The rest of the field was left far behind, in a different race. His switch to slicks was timed to perfection and his unruffled progress continued until mid-way round lap 39. Then the oil warning light flickered momentarily.

'I had one lap warning,' he said later. 'The red light came on, so I knew something was going on. Finally, next time round, the engine seized and lost power. I was absolutely flat out coming through the tunnel and there was tons of oil all over the track and rear wheels.

'I locked up and just managed to park it. I'm gutted, because I had a big gap and I was working to make it bigger in case I needed to stop again. I just hope this isn't going to be too costly for my championship chances.' The failure was subsequently traced to melting adhesive on an oil pump lock nut.

It was a bitter blow for Damon, and a taste of things to come. A fortnight later his grand plan continued to come unstitched in a rain-soaked Spanish GP at Barcelona which was won by Schumacher in heroic, historic style. Indeed, it was the stuff of legends, ranking alongside Ayrton Senna's dazzling performance at Donington Park on a dank Easter Sunday three years before.

Tactical error. Damon slumps from pole to third behind Villeneuve and Alesi as the pack battles in the murk seconds after the start of the 1996 Spanish GP. Handicapped by an over-stiff chassis set-up, Damon spun out early on (ICN UK Bureau).

The bare facts are that Michael scored his first victory for Maranello by the margin of 45sec over Jean Alesi's Benetton-Renault. As a stark counterpoint, having started on pole, Hill found himself out-accelerated by Jacques Villeneuve and Jean Alesi from the start, then spun twice before pirouetting into the pit wall coming off the last corner at the start of lap 11.

The contrast in fortunes between the two key championship players was remarkable. Schumacher again displayed his genius, but Hill took the inexplicable decision to start with a compromise wet/dry chassis set-up, hoping that a dry line would begin to appear as the race progressed

'I made three mistakes and had the wrong set-up on the car,' he admitted. 'It was really down to me what happened today. The big problem (in these conditions) is visibility. At the end of the first lap I went down the straight and there were cars on the right and people working on one on the left, and I didn't see them until I was on top of them. You just cannot see the road ahead at all.

'This was a bad day for the championship. I made a bad start, but I reckon I am as good as anyone in the wet and will have to work out why I didn't go well today.' Hill now had 43 points, with Villeneuve and Schumacher tying for second place on 26 apiece.

After qualifying Hill had already made his opinion known on the subject of Renault's current state of engine development:

'I am not happy with the engines, I have to say. I had an engine blow in testing (last week at Silverstone) and Jacques had another one here today. It is a problem of which we and Renault are well aware. To win, we need two things – reliability is something for which Renault has become famous, but we also need some performance'.

Such observations were probably not best timed as, behind the scenes, Renault was carefully considering its F1 future. Only a few more weeks would pass before the French company announced that it would withdraw from Grand Prix racing at the end of 1997, a decision which would leave both Williams and Benetton looking for new technical partners.

There is not even the hint of a suggestion that Damon's complaints were a factor behind Renault's decision to quit, the evidence being that the strategy had been decided on several months earlier. Taking a wider view, and considering the engine/car combination as a whole, Damon admitted that he was delighted with the technical package which had been placed at his disposal for the 1996 season.

'It is a beautiful car to work with because it responds to all the changes we make to it and that gives us a very good opportunity to

Right *A job to be done. A study in concentration prior to the start of the 1996 French Grand Prix* (Darren Heath).

Blue skies, nothing but blue skies. Damon was unchallenged in France after Schumacher's pole-winning Ferrari suffered engine failure on the formation lap (Darren Heath).

balance it out for each circuit we go to,' he explained.

'The aerodynamics and engineering on the FW18 are superb. It is a tremendous piece of equipment, and every time I drive the car I enjoy playing with it. I can really adapt and experiment with it. That's great.'

The disappointments of Monaco and Spain were soon reversed in convincing style when Damon bounced back onto winning form in the Canadian GP at Montreal. A well-judged victory over team-mate Jacques Villeneuve on the evocatively titled Circuit Gilles Villeneuve — named after Jacques's legendary father — was as good a way as any for Damon to celebrate the season's halfway point.

Damon thus reasserted his position at the head of the championship points table with 53 points to the German's 26. Mathematically more concerning for him was the fact that Villeneuve scored a third place in

Spain and a second before his home crowd to move into second place with 32 points. It seemed that the strongest challenge to Hill's title prospects now could well come from within his own team.

Damon qualified on pole position in Montreal, everything went faultlessly, and he exerted a commanding early advantage by dint of a two stop strategy in contrast to Villeneuve's one stop plan of campaign. Schumacher's hopes of making it a three-way fight evaporated at the start when his Ferrari F310 — revamped with a distinctive Williams-style high nose for the first time — suffered fuel pressure problems on the grid, was late away on the parade lap and had to start at the back of the 20-car pack.

Plagued thereafter by erratic brake balance, he climbed to seventh place before making his one scheduled refuelling stop only for a driveshaft to fracture and fly out of the back of the car as he accelerated away again. It ensured he was posted as a retirement on a day which saw team-mate Eddie Irvine succumb to a broken front suspension push-rod. It was Ferrari's lowest moment of the year so far.

125

Bad start at home. Jacques Villeneuve's Williams takes an early lead at Silverstone as Hill (out of picture to right) fumbles another pole position (ICN UK Bureau).

After the race, Schumacher made a great play of conceding the title to Hill, but Frank Williams shrugged aside such pessimistic predictions from the German wunderkind. 'Michael would remain a formidable challenge if he was only driving a pram,' he said. Damon simply remarked, 'I don't think we've seen the end of Michael'.

Perhaps so, but Schumacher's outside challenge for a third World Championship faded dramatically in July with the Ferrari team's absolutely disastrous outings in the French and British Grands Prix. Yet fortunes change quickly in this game. Only a fortnight after Damon Hill won the Magny-Cours race, notching up a 25 point advantage over Villeneuve, he suddenly found himself facing a brisk title challenge from the Indycar ace who won his second F1 victory at Silverstone – and settled a score with Hill about being beaten at his own home race in Canada.

Hill's decisive win at Magny-Cours was inevitably overshadowed by Renault making public its decision to quit F1 at the end of 1997. Frenzied speculation that Honda and BMW could step in to replace the French engine supplier did not take long to start circulating in the paddock.

In France, Schumacher qualified brilliantly on pole only for his V10 engine to suffer piston failure on the formation lap. His team-mate

126

Eddie Irvine, who had been relegated to the back of the grid after his car's aerodynamic deflectors were found to infringe the technical rules in qualifying, lasted only five laps before the gearbox hydraulics packed up.

Despite an intensive test programme at Monza in the break between the French and British races, Maranello's depressing run continued at Silverstone where Ferrari President Luca di Montezemolo was joined by Fiat patriarch Gianni Agnelli for the first day's practice. Montezemolo was his usual positive self, talking in terms of extending Schumacher's contract beyond a second year into 1998, but most F1 insiders came away from the British Grand Prix realising that the German driver held all the negotiating cards and could delay any decision about his future for at least another 12 months.

In the short term, Schumacher wanted to forget his visit to Silverstone as quickly as possible. With two of the race's 61 laps completed, his Ferrari was limping towards the pits jammed in sixth gear thanks to a terminal hydraulic leak. Irvine checked out a few laps later with differential failure, bringing the curtain down on another nightmare weekend for the Prancing Horse. 'This is absurd,' shrugged an exasperated Schumacher.

In the meantime, things were going little better for Britain's hometown hero. Hill had qualified on pole, fractionally ahead of team-mate Villeneuve. After fluffing his start, he completed the opening lap in fifth place and was running third on lap 27, poised to make his first refuelling stop, when the FW18 suddenly snapped away from him and he spun into the gravel trap at Copse corner.

This inelegant pirouette into retirement – caused by a loose front wheel nut – was definitely not his fault, as BBC viewers were advised more than several times by Murray Walker and Jonathan Palmer.

'I had a sensation at the front of the car for three or four laps, perhaps suspecting that the front anti-roll bar had broken,' Hill explained, 'and finally I got on the radio and told the pits I thought I had a problem. Then, as I was going into Copse, it felt as though something seized at the front. I didn't make a good start, but all was not lost as I was within 20 seconds of Jacques and could have changed to a two stop strategy.'

With Hill out, Villeneuve was left to uphold Williams team honour on his own, a task he performed admirably to narrow Damon's points lead from 25 to 15. Unfortunately the afternoon – already a disappointment for the crowds of devoted Hill fans – ended on an unpleasant note when Benetton protested the legality of the Williams front wing endplates.

This protest left Williams design chiefs Patrick Head and Adrian Newey fuming with indignation. There were even suggestions, vigorously rebutted by Flavio Briatore, that Benetton's management

Not my day. After spinning off due to a loose front wheel nut, Damon returns to the Williams pit, his 1996 British GP at a premature and unexpected end (ICN UK Bureau).

had been put up to it by Ferrari as an indirect means of paying Williams back for drawing added attention to the dimensional irregularities with Ferrari's aerodynamic deflectors during practice for the French Grand Prix.

The Williams design and engineering staff was emphatically unamused at the protest, clearly feeling that it was vexatious and personal. The atmosphere between the representatives of the rival teams could be cut with a knife as stewards deliberated over the matter. However, after a lengthy debate, the Benetton protest was rejected and the point made that the FIA technical delegate Charlie Whiting had regarded the wings as legal from the start of the season. Benetton, most people felt, had been guilty of wasting the officials' time.

Villeneuve's victory at Silverstone virtually clinched for Williams the 1996 Constructors' Championship beyond all but the most remote mathematical possibility. Gerhard Berger did well to finish second for Benetton, adding to his fourth place in France, while Mika Hakkinen was third in the much-improved McLaren-Mercedes MP4/11 which had qualified fourth on the grid only 0.9sec away from Damon's pole position Williams.

For Damon, of course, the picture was slightly different. Now he was only 15 points ahead of Jacques Villeneuve with six races of the season still to run. Any examination of the situation would have concluded that he retained the upper hand – particularly bearing in mind that Jacques had no prior experience at Hockenheim, Hungaroring or Spa, the next three races on the schedule – but it was all getting a little too tight for comfort.

There were also other rumblings on the horizon. The time for renegotiating contracts was approaching – F1's traditional 'silly season' – and media speculation went into top gear as the teams prepared for Hockenheim. Earlier in the summer, Damon had announced, with what turned out to be a poignant accuracy, that he would be 'footloose and fancy-free' at the end of the year when his Williams contract expired, but privately there was no doubt in his mind that he wanted to stay with the team if he won the championship. Assuming, of course, that the price was right.

It was therefore with a degree of disappointment that Damon arrived at Hockenheim to be presented with the latest copy of *Autosport* magazine emblazoned with the cover line 'Has Hill been dumped by Williams?'

This was the trailer for a lead story to the effect that Frank Williams had already decided to replace Hill for 1997, and was to sign a firm contract with the German driver Heinz-Harald Frentzen to partner Villeneuve.

The story was based round the assertion of a leading F1 figure – who preferred to remain anonymous – who was quoted as saying that Frentzen was definite for Williams. Yet Frank Williams immediately denied that Frentzen had been signed. 'I will start serious talks with Damon and his representatives within the next few weeks,' he said. 'At the present time I only have Villeneuve signed for 1997.'

It was said that Hill's demand for $10 million was being dismissed

It was being speculated that Hill's demands for a pay rise to around $10 million had already effectively been dismissed by Williams at Silverstone. Nevertheless, Hill's lawyer Michael Breen said he was confident that a deal could be struck with Williams and doubted the team had any commitment to Frentzen.

'I think it is fanciful speculation,' said Breen. 'Damon has won six races and is well on the way to the World Championship. Williams want a number one on their car and so I would obviously like to start soon on negotiating a deal for 1997.

'Damon had made it quite clear that he wants more money if he is World Champion, and Frank has indicated that he is prepared to pay more. It is a question of establishing where the line is drawn.'

Meanwhile, Frentzen's manager Ortwin Podlech admitted that he was working to secure a deal with Williams, but that there was no progress yet.

'It is just nonsense to suggest that Frank has an option on Heinz-Harald's services,' said Podlech. 'Why would he need an option? Any driver without a contract – and some with one – would run the length of the paddock and camp in front of the Williams transporter if they thought there was a chance of a drive!' It was a pithy observation which seemed to carry more than a ring of truth.

Podlech also confirmed that Frentzen had been in talks with the Jordan-Peugeot team for much of the year, but would not comment on the rumour that he had cancelled a meeting with Eddie Jordan over the Hockenheim weekend in order to continue negotiations with Williams.

For his part, Hill reacted stoically. 'I haven't bothered to read any newspapers,' he shrugged. 'The only thing I have to say is that Frank and I are united in a common goal, to win the Drivers' and Constructors' Championships for Williams. I am very, very happy at the moment, I've come direct from Ricard testing where things went very well.

A lot of our success has been because of my own hard work and application

'You will all be informed what I'm doing next year. Winning the championship would obviously give me a lot of options, and that's what I'm trying to do. But I'm not going to be drawn into discussing my future in Grand Prix racing.'

However, he did not deny that staying with Williams was the main priority. 'I think I've made that plain many times before,' he said. 'I feel very much a part of the team and that a lot of the success we've had this year has been brought about by my hard work and application, and by being a good team member. And I don't want that to change.'

After qualifying on pole position at Hockenheim, it had looked as though Hill might again be in trouble as he made a slow start and completed the opening lap third behind the Benettons of Berger and Alesi. This trio quickly pulled away from the rest of the pack which was initially headed by Michael Schumacher's Ferrari which had also lost ground when the German driver tried to squeeze Mika Hakkinen's McLaren against the pit wall as they accelerated away from the grid.

Hill was scheduled to make two refuelling stops, but had sufficient fuel from the start to have maximum tactical flexibility as to when he pitted for the first time. Having satisfied himself that both the Benettons ahead were likely to be stopping once, he came in at the end of lap 20 and was thus able to emerge in the lead after Alesi and Berger made their sole stops shortly afterwards.

Now it was down to Hill to open out sufficient of a cushion to allow himself to emerge from his second refuelling stop without losing the lead. Between lap 26 and 34, when he finally came in, he stretched his advantage over Berger from 6.2sec to 15.9sec before coming back into

Business as usual. Damon explains how he took pole position for the 1996 German GP at Hockenheim (ICN UK Bureau).

the pits for his second stop. Unfortunately that short spell under the yellow flag, warning of a slower car in front, just tipped the advantage back in Berger's favour and Hill emerged a couple of seconds behind the Benetton for the sprint to the finish.

There followed a frenzied battle between Hill and Berger which was only resolved a couple of laps from the chequered flag when the Austrian suffered a massive engine failure while running a few yards ahead of his English rival.

'I was pushing him hard and hoping he would make a mistake,' said Hill. 'It was always going to be a big risk to try and pass him, and I had to bear that in mind. I meant to score points, but I wanted to win.'

Hill crossed the finishing line 11.4 seconds ahead of Alesi and Villeneuve, his only remaining title challenger. Schumacher was fortunate to scramble home fourth after a battle with David Coulthard's fifth place McLaren-Mercedes. Having won here 12 months earlier, now watching Hill take another stride towards relieving him of his World Championship crown was a bitter pill for Schumacher to swallow. And like Villeneuve's massive following in Canada, and Hill's devoted home crowd at Silverstone, the 150,000 Schumacher fans were understandably disconsolate too.

Damon made it clear that he did not regard Hockenheim as a lucky win: 'Absolutely no way. I have had my fair share of bad luck here. Unfortunately these things happen in motor racing – and the last few laps would have been exciting if Gerhard had kept going.

'I came out of the Clark chicane and suddenly heard one of our engines make a strange noise. I thought it might be mine, but Gerhard moved slightly to the left and I dodged right just before it erupted.

'I won't deny that Gerhard's failure to finish was fortuitous, but these things happen. If it had not been for the fact that I lost a couple of seconds passing yellow warning flags before my second pit stop, I would have got out of the pits ahead of him for the last time and the race would have been in the bag.'

Silverstone re-run. Hill makes a poor start in Germany, allowing the Benettons of Gerhard Berger and Jean Alesi to snatch an early lead. Unlike at Silverstone, however, Damon recovered to notch up another victory when Berger's engine expired with a couple of laps to go (ICN UK Bureau).

Hill's success at last broke a three-year run of misfortune in the German race. In 1993, he had been heading for victory in front of Williams team-mate Alain Prost when a rear tyre punctured just over a mile from the finish. In 1994, he bent a steering arm in a first lap collision, and last year he spun into a gravel trap while leading at the start of the second lap.

As he emerged from the German GP with his seventh win out of 11 races so far, he had extended his advantage to 21 points over Villeneuve with 50 left to play for over the five remaining races of the year. It was also his 20th Grand Prix win, matching his German rival's own much-vaunted tally.

Hill's confidence about his future F1 career arrangements was brought into sharp focus in the immediate aftermath of the German Grand Prix. It seemed likely that the influence of television coverage might well be the key factor behind the scenes which would guarantee Damon a renewal of his contract with Williams for 1997,

particularly with the championship now virtually in his sights.

At the end of a weekend when Hill had displayed a consistently cheerful insouciance in response to the Frentzen rumours, it emerged that ITV's recently signed £65 million, five-year deal needed Hill in a front-running car to maximise their advertising revenue.

It was known that ITV only made its bid after examining in detail the excellent ratings gained by the BBC. With ITV's market profile driven by cars, telecommunications and finance, it regarded high-profile live events such as the F1 World Championship as crucial to its business.

Andrew Chowns, the man responsible for negotiating the ITV deal with FIA vice president Bernie Ecclestone, admitted before Hockenheim that having a top British driver in a winning car was a significant consideration. 'When Hill retired from the British Grand Prix, the viewing figures dropped,' he said.

Ecclestone obviously appreciated this point, but firmly denied rumours circulating at Hockenheim that he had sought to pressure Frank Williams on the question of retaining Hill's services. 'It would be good to have Damon in any top car,' he said, 'but I would never seek to influence the Williams team on this matter. It is absolutely Frank's decision.'

However, he did later add: 'I do not imagine for one minute that Damon is worth less next year. He would be the World Champion, which helps him gain sponsors, and has done a bloody good job.

'I do not think for one moment that Frank will get rid of him. Maybe he is asking for a fortune, but if he is prepared to drive for what he has this year, then that would be good for Damon and good for Frank.' The strong implication behind these words was that Damon might have been slightly overpaid in 1996 and so it might be acceptable to balance that out by slightly underpaying him in 1997. This didn't seem to be an idea which would meet with Damon's unreserved approval.

Yet perhaps these remarks reflected an underlying reservation about Hill's degree of natural talent. For example, Ken Tyrrell was one of many who confessed that he was initially surprised at the level of success which Damon had achieved in F1.

'Yes, I was,' he said at Hockenheim in 1996. 'Prior to F1, he hadn't done anything. We looked hard at his times when he was driving the Brabham and the young Belgian lad, van de Poele, was mostly quicker.

'I think Damon has done it the same way as his Dad did. I don't think Graham had any great talent, but he won Monaco five times as well as Indianapolis and Le Mans. Damon has slogged away at it. He's not a Clark, a Senna or a Stewart, but he's done a great job. All credit to him.'

However, while there were certainly many rivals who would give their shirt for a Williams drive, a glance back in recent F1 history certainly made it appropriate to sound a cautionary note. With the 1997 season scheduled to be Renault's last as the Williams team's engine suppliers, it was clearly questionable whether or not the French company could sustain its technical edge.

Back in 1992, Honda rounded off a partnership with McLaren which had produced four straight World Championships with a dismal season in which even the great Ayrton Senna was hard-pressed to win races. Ironically, Honda's decline coincided with the rise of the Williams-Renaults.

After four seasons at the top, Williams had to be mindful of the fact that history could repeat itself. If the baton should pass to another team, Damon Hill's value to Williams might end up being calculated not in terms of what he could do in the best car, but what results he might produce in one which was merely competitive.

After Hockenheim it was clear that Damon needed to refine his starting technique as a matter of some urgency if he was to give himself the best chance of winning the Hungarian Grand Prix at the Hungaroring, near Budapest, which is one of the tightest tracks on the F1 trail.

Hill needed to refine his starting technique as a matter of urgency

In both the past two races he had made a poor start from pole position. He knew he must not squander any such advantage in Sunday's race. 'Yes, it has been more difficult to get the car off the line. The characteristics of the 3-litre engines are different to the old 3.5-litre engines: they don't have so much torque. It is an area we are working on.'

Having won at the Hungaroring twice before, in 1993 and 1995, Hill knew better than most that overtaking there almost totally depended on the driver in front making a mistake. (Back in 1990 Thierry Boutsen won the race for Williams by less than a length ahead of Ayrton Senna's McLaren by the simple virtue of keeping cool and not allowing himself to be pressured into an error. The fact that Senna was running two seconds a lap quicker than his Belgian rival mattered not one jot once he pulled up onto the tail of the Williams. He could not get past.)

Hill completed the first Hungarian GP free practice session with fastest time, ahead of Villeneuve and Schumacher, both of whom could prove impossibly tough nuts to crack if they got a sniff of the lead.

'I am quite surprised to be as quick as we were,' said Damon. 'We started off with a good (chassis) set-up, we made some good changes, and we have a lot of things we can think about overnight.

'There is certainly a small feel-good factor about this circuit for me. It's a circuit I feel familiar with, but Jacques has done a very good job to get so close on the first day. He is certainly raring to go.'

Villeneuve went into the race 21 points behind Hill with 50 still to fight for over the five remaining races. Although the odds seemed clearly stacked against him, Villeneuve was absolutely determined to keep the pressure on his partner right through to the end of the season.

The young Canadian's speed on his first ever outing at Hungaroring certainly impressed many onlookers, yet the strongest challenge seemed likely to come from Schumacher. The Ferraris were looking good – Schumacher's team-mate Eddie Irvine emerged from the first session with fourth fastest time.

'For sure I am more or less on the same performance level as the Williams,' said the German. 'But it is important to underline that I did less laps than them, and so my tyres were slightly better when I set my quick time.'

Damon felt upbeat and optimistic about his prospects. He was going for a win. That was all that interested him:

'I think at this stage of the championship it's obviously better to be in front – 21 points is a healthy lead. On the other hand, five races are still quite a considerable number, effectively one-third of the championship. I think the temptation after Hockenheim was to assume that, well, I've gone forward and stretched the lead, and it is tempting to think everything is settled. But of course it is not.

'The Hungarian GP is a race I enjoy. I won my first Grand Prix here, and I won again last year. In fact, I had a great race in 1995, a particularly good race from the viewpoint that I was under pressure all the time. Michael gave me a good challenge and I still came out ahead'.

Damon would not make any comment as far as his professional future was concerned. 'I don't have anything more to add. Of course I have had talks with Frank Williams. It is an ongoing discussion and, while I think things are going well on that front, it is not the main topic on my mind at the moment.

'I really have only one thing on my mind, to try and win each race I go to. That's the way I have been operating. I relaxed between Hockenheim and Hungary, without driving at all. It was nice to get out of the car and stand back a bit from it all. I've been having a bit of a holiday in the south of France with my family and the children, getting away from the pressures and the travel.'

Did Damon believe he would feel under less pressure at Hungary because his team-mate Jacques Villeneuve had no experience of the circuit? 'Again, it's tempting to think that, but I am wary of falling into that trap. I don't think I've been to a circuit this year where Jacques has not been, at some point or other, a contender. He is improving all the time; he knows the car very well now; he knows the set-up and the operation. Give somebody 60 or 70 laps on a new circuit before a race and they've probably learned all they need to about the place.'

For the rest of the season Damon also anticipated that he would face an increasing challenge from the Benetton-Renault team. He did not regard their Hockenheim performance as a one-off.

'I think they have made some progress. They showed a little bit of improvement when they went testing at Paul Ricard, just before the German GP, and I was quite surprised by their pace. They kept that going through the race weekend, and Hockenheim certainly showed that we had no advantage on the engine front. If they have made a step forward with the chassis, it might be expected to be showing up on a circuit like Hungaroring.'

Damon again emphasised that there was no way in which he could rely on Villeneuve to support him in his own title quest. 'It would be lovely to have a situation where there was no rivalry within your own team. That would be quite cosy. But that's not the situation. We have a free hand to race against each other. He wants to win badly, and so do I. But that doesn't mean I'm yet racing tactically. Having said that, at Hockenheim I was certainly mindful of the fact that I wanted to finish and that Gerhard would probably do anything to stay in front right to the end.

'At all the races for the moment, my objective is to win. Seeing that far into a race, to a situation where I might be ready to settle for points, is not something which I have yet envisaged.'

More points slipping. Michael Schumacher had already accelerated his Ferrari out of the frame at the start of the 1996 Hungarian GP, while Jacques Villeneuve (leading here) is in second place with Jean Alesi's Benetton about to take third from Hill's Williams. The day ended with Villeneuve another four points closer in the title chase (ICN UK Bureau).

Another disappointment. Damon en route to fifth place in the Belgian GP. Another four points lost to the second-placed Villeneuve (ICN UK Bureau).

So did he feel it was important to have the objective of trying to beat Nigel Mansell's record of nine wins in a season? 'Well, it's good to win on a roll. I've got seven this year at the moment, and every possibility of adding to them between now and the end of the season. But I'm not thinking about that record as an objective – I'm just out to win as many races as I can.'

Frustratingly, the outcome of the Hungarian GP simply served to leave Hill's championship hopes under further assault. Villeneuve beat him into second place. In a tactically demanding and complex battle, Hill had rejoined after his third refuelling stop 7sec behind his rival. He reduced that to 0.7sec – three car lengths – over the remaining 15 laps to the chequered flag, but there was simply no way past.

Villeneuve's third victory in his freshman F1 season reduced Hill's

points advantage to only 17, with four races to go.

Behind Hill, Jean Alesi's Benetton finished third, almost lapped by the dominant Williams duo, and Mika Hakkinen's McLaren, Olivier Panis's Ligier, and the Jordan of Rubens Barrichello completed the top half dozen. Schumacher, having qualified on pole, went out with throttle problems while running third with only seven laps left to go.

Hill effectively lost the race when he was slow away from second place on the front row of the grid, having to race off-line on the dust as the pack sprinted for the first corner. While Villeneuve completed the opening lap tucked tightly behind Schumacher's leading Ferrari, Hill was bogged down in fourth place behind Jean Alesi, a setback which cost him a second a lap in the early stage of the race.

'I was particularly disgusted at the start,' admitted Hill. 'But that aside, the race was a very good one. I had to push like mad to catch up, make the gap. In the closing stages I was the fastest car on the lap, but I lost the race behind Jean in the first 10 laps. Michael and Jacques were long gone.

'The way the clutch works doesn't suit me, and I have been working very hard to try and get a clutch I can use more easily. But we're going testing in Barcelona, where we can do some more work on that. I'm really frustrated about the way it operates. I don't know how many times the clutch has cost me time at the start of the race.'

Having made that slow start, Hill believed he would have been better served with a two stop strategy rather than the three stops he eventually ended up with. 'When I made the first stop I thought I was doing a two stop until the time I came in for my second stop and then I found out I was doing another stop. So it was a bit confusing.'

In fact, when Schumacher came in for his first refuelling stop, Hill stayed out for another six laps in order to make sufficient ground on the Ferrari to try to get ahead of it as he emerged from his own first stop. He dropped to fourth behind Alesi, only overtaking for third place on lap 31 of the 77 lap race when the Frenchman slid wide at the first corner.

By this point Villeneuve had managed to slip ahead of Schumacher to take the lead during the first round of refuelling stops, after which Hill only got one chance to make a realistic challenge when the Canadian lost 10sec at his final refuelling stop with a sticking rear wheel nut.

In the closing stages Villeneuve did all he needed to, concentrating on keeping things tidy and not making a mistake. Although Hill was easily the fastest car on the circuit at this stage of the race, Villeneuve refused to be pressured and rounded off the afternoon confident that he could make Damon work for the championship right through to the final race at Suzuka.

However, while the outcome of the drivers' championship still remained finely balanced between their two drivers after the Hungarian race, the Williams team ended the day having clinched its eighth constructors' title. This equalled Ferrari's record, although the Italian marque won its first such title in 1961, 19 years before the British team posted its maiden triumph.

Ironically, two weeks later after Hungary it would be Hill's arch rival Michael Schumacher who did him a rare favour by beating Villeneuve into second place in the Belgian Grand Prix at Spa-Francorchamps.

The Ferrari driver's brilliant performance on this high-speed track looked likely to be a crucial factor in enabling Hill to scrape home with the World Championship after two disappointing races in which the momentum definitely seemed to have passed to Villeneuve. Damon finished fifth. He frankly counted himself lucky that he had lost only another three points to his team-mate, to emerge from the weekend with a 13 point lead with three rounds left.

'It was a relief to get two points,' said Hill. 'I thought that Jacques might win, and I was not going to get any points at all at one time, but I have to admit that 13 points is not what I would call a comfortable lead in the championship.

Jean Alesi's Benetton leads through the first chicane after the start of the Italian GP at Monza. Hill is tight on his tail while Villeneuve takes to the grass. Later Jacques would accuse Damon of failing to give him sufficient room (ICN UK Bureau).

'But I am not despondent, even though it was not the race I had hoped for, and the car was not as quick as it should have been. We did not have the handling balance I had enjoyed during practice and qualifying, and I think the team under-performed as a whole.'

From the start Villeneuve had taken an immediate lead ahead of Schumacher who had burst through from the second row to take second place in front of Hill. The Englishman's problems were then compounded when David Coulthard's impressive McLaren-Mercedes surged past into third place on the 190mph climb to the Les Combes corner.

Hill found himself battling with a serious handling imbalance on his first set of tyres but settled down to run fourth in the opening stages, although he was steadily dropping away from the leaders.

However, his real difficulties loomed as the field bunched up in tight formation when the safety car was deployed to slow the pack following a spectacular accident to Jos Verstappen's Footwork-Hart. The Williams team fumbled. A problem with the radio communication between Villeneuve's car and the pit crew meant that Jacques did not hear instructions to come in to refuel at the end of lap 14 as intended.

He stayed out and came in the following lap, scrambling the team's refuelling plans as Hill was on schedule to come in this time round. The

Ending in tears. Damon clipped a tyre barrier and spun off while leading the early stages at Monza. It was a potentially disastrous blow to his title chances (ICN UK Bureau).

team just managed to instruct Damon to stay out for another lap, but he had to dodge through the barriers in the pit entrance lane and lost a lot of time before finally coming in at the end of the following lap.

By the time he resumed the chase, Hill was well down the field with a huge gaggle of slightly slower cars just ahead of him. By lap 20 he was up to ninth, then fifth by lap 25, before dropping back to sixth after his second refuelling stop on lap 34.

In the closing stages Schumacher eased away from Villeneuve who was also suffering from understeer on his final set of tyres, and the reigning World Champion eventually took the chequered flag with just over 5sec in hand over the hard-driven Williams. Schumacher finished the day privately acknowledging that Villeneuve was one of the most formidable rivals he had faced.

Yet Frank Williams sounded a cautionary note about the future: 'If Ferrari gets on top of its reliability problems over the winter, which it will, then Michael could disappear next season'.

For Hill, fighting an increasingly uphill battle for a place in the sun with his first World Championship title, those words offered scant encouragement.

Senior Williams personnel were now privately quite worried. Frank Williams had said on several occasions that he was keen to sign Hill, but there were no firm warning signals on the horizon. Hill's solicitor Michael Breen would later describe Damon as a 'very fine racing driver with 20 wins to his credit', but that was only part of the story. Whichever way

Hill and his advisors viewed the situation, his 1996 World Championship challenge was becoming slightly frayed at the edges.

Heinz-Harald Frentzen had started out in Frank's mind as a likely driver for 1997. Then Hill performed so well in the opening phase of the 1996 season that it finally seemed as if he was a different man. However that recent spate of poor starts began to tell another story. Damon was fine out on his own in the lead. But he was not quite so impressive in traffic. The old reservations about his performance under pressure were resurfacing. With a vengeance.

A brief telephone call at 12.10 on Wednesday, 28 August brought Damon Hill's career as a Williams F1 driver to an end after six years and 20 Grand Prix wins. The timing and manner of his dismissal stunned the outside world. Most of the top drives were already signed for 1997. Where was Hill to go at this late stage – and how would he be treated for the rest of this season by a team understandably keen to have the coveted Number 1 on its own car next year?

In the call, Frank Williams had reportedly politely informed Michael Breen that he was withdrawing from the contractual negotiations which had been continuing for a couple of weeks. Apart from explaining that the reason behind his decision had nothing to do with money, Williams offered Breen no other explanation.

'It was a bolt from the blue,' said Breen. 'When we were negotiating for this season, Frank said to Damon "let's see what happens: if you win the championship, you know I have already lost enough World Champions and been berated by my sponsors that I would never ever do it again". Is that good enough?'

Williams was referring to Nigel Mansell's departure under acrimonious circumstances in 1992, followed by Alain Prost's retirement a year later when Ayrton Senna was recruited against his will. Both men left Williams as reigning World Champions.

The news hardly came as a shock to many on the inside of the Formula 1 business. They had been waiting for just such an announcement for several days. Yet the timing could hardly have been worse, putting Hill under even more pressure as he sought to protect his 13 point lead from team-mate Jacques Villeneuve in the Italian GP at Monza.

What Williams most certainly did not say was that there had never been any real chance of signing Hill for 1997 because he had long ago completed a deal for the German driver Heinz-Harald Frentzen to race alongside Jacques Villeneuve next season. This scenario had been consistently denied by the team.

Frank Williams confined himself to the barest of formalities with a bland statement that signalled he would not become involved in a media debate over how he sacked the best British F1 driver since Nigel Mansell.

It was suggested that Williams might have been slightly irked by Breen's negotiating style. On the other hand, Breen had been dealing with Hill's business affairs for many years and was responsible for negotiating the excellent retainer – reputedly £5 million – which Damon had enjoyed in 1996. More likely, Williams was worried that Hill's sequence of poor starts and apparent inability to overtake, would leave the team at a serious disadvantage in the event of a dramatic Schumacher renaissance in 1997.

'Damon is disappointed and saddened,' said Breen with masterly understatement at a media conference in the Conrad Hotel at London's Chelsea Harbour on 1 September.

'To set the record straight, we only began negotiations with Frank Williams in mid-August. Obviously there were several points on the table. On Wednesday, August 28th Frank called me and said that he was withdrawing from talks about the contract and would not be taking it any further, giving no reasons for this decision.

'With regards to the future, I wouldn't be doing my job if I had not already been looking for the best drive for Damon in 1997. Discussions are under way to find him the most attractive position in which he will be both happy and appreciated for the next few seasons.'

Williams said that his decision had nothing to do with money. But it was known that Hill had been hoping to get an increase on his £5 million retainer – and that Williams had signalled a degree of concern that he might have to pay for his engine supply in 1998 after Renault withdrew from F1.

The plot thickened further. It began to look likely that Hill would revive an old partnership with Eddie Jordan. On the day following Breen's press conference, Jordan confirmed that the team had already held talks with him and would be doing so again in the near future.

Hill had driven for Eddie Jordan's Formula 3000 team back in 1991, six years after the Irishman gave him his first Formula 3 test outing in one of his cars.

Jordan's commercial manager Ian Phillips admitted that Hill could be the ideal candidate to help raise the team's profile and please both Benson & Hedges, its key sponsor, as well as its French engine suppliers:

'We are amazed that Damon has been released by Williams and, up to the weekend, hadn't even considered he would be available for 1997. Now that he is, we must reappraise our situation and possible plans'.

Of course, Hill's value to any new team might risk being devalued if he failed to clinch the World Championship. One possibility soon floated was that Damon might join Gerhard Berger at Benetton in a

Right Up and away. Hill leads the start of the Portuguese GP at Estoril. He built up a commanding early lead, only for Villeneuve to demolish it and score a brilliant victory in one of the season's most remarkable reversals of form (ICN UK Bureau).

transfer engineered by Renault who were initially said to be dismayed by Frank Williams's decision.

Yet Benetton team chief Flavio Briatore moved to cool speculation about such a move which would involve buying off Jean Alesi's contract to the end of 1997 and engineering the Frenchman's switch to the Jordan-Peugeot team.

'Damon has not so many possibilities,' said Briatore at Monza. 'Benetton is closed, McLaren is closed, Ferrari is closed. I suppose it could be different if he came with the Number 1, but he is not in good shape.

'With Schumacher confirmed at Ferrari, I see no better driver pairing for 1997 than Alesi and Berger. They are quick, work well together and work well with the team. I have no intention of changing for 1997. The priority for Benetton today is not the recruitment of new drivers, it is to improve our chassis.'

Meanwhile, Eddie Jordan's comments continued to fuel speculation that he was favourite to sign Hill. 'We would be delighted to have Damon in the team. He is a fantastically professional person, he has won 20 grands prix and he is about as fine a gentleman as you could meet, both on and off the track. It would be a big boost for Jordan if he was to come to us. That is my very personal opinion.'

Whichever team he eventually drove for, the prospect of seeing Hill in something other than a Williams certainly fascinated Michael Schumacher:

'When Damon wins a race some people, me included, think "well, how good is he?" So I think that changing to another team next year offers him an opportunity to prove he is better than some people might think. We might get a surprise in that respect, and then we know how good he is and how good is his car'.

Not that the Italian Grand Prix proved much of a sales pitch for Hill. He threw away an easy victory with an absurd spin on the sixth lap — but then watched with relief as Villeneuve only managed to hobble home seventh, passing up a golden opportunity to reduce his title points deficit.

That left the way clear for Michael Schumacher to celebrate Ferrari's third victory of the season, much to the joy of the passionate 100,000-strong crowd. Michael trailed Jean Alesi's Benetton in the opening stages of the race, then vaulted ahead at their sole refuelling stops to break the Frenchman's challenge with a series of crushingly fast laps in the closing stages.

Hill was disarmingly candid about the lapse which saw him clip one of the makeshift tyre barriers erected to stop drivers clipping the kerbs at the first and second chicanes. The tail of his Williams snapped out to the left and he was unable to catch it. He spun and stalled in front of the pack.

'I could have finished it off today,' said Hill, reflecting on his still

Putting a smile on it. Damon celebrates second place on the rostrum at Estoril (ICN UK Bureau).

pending World Championship business. 'I was having a really stonking good race, a really good, aggressive start – the car was really stretching its legs.

'I can offer no explanation for what happened other than I didn't concentrate hard enough. It was probably the easiest race victory I could have picked up, but I threw it away. I can't blame anybody but myself.'

Then came the Portuguese Grand Prix. This was a race which Hill led from the start and again it seemed certain to provide him with the opportunity to clinch the title. Yet he was beaten into second place by Villeneuve and ended the afternoon a single point short of the title crown.

From the moment he accelerated away from pole position on the starting grid, Hill had looked in complete control. By the time he pulled in for his first routine refuelling stop at the end of lap 17, he was 8.8sec sec ahead of Jean Alesi's second placed Benetton.

Yet the next few laps would again serve to underline the nagging reservations which the Williams team have privately harboured over the completeness of his driving repertoire. His performance when it comes to carving through heavy traffic yet again proved his most obvious Achilles heel and, almost imperceptibly, the spring tide of his advantage started to ebb away.

Looking thoughtful. After their 1–2 finish in the Portuguese GP, Jacques Villeneuve is already out of the cockpit of his Williams in the scrutineering area. Hill, a beaten second, still sits in his car looking pensive (ICN UK Bureau).

At the end of lap 20, Hill was running second behind Jean Alesi's Benetton, some 19.846sec ahead of Villeneuve who was in fourth place behind Mika Hakkinen's McLaren. Hill had just turned a lap in 1m 24.944s, Villeneuve in 1m 23.902s.

On lap 21, Hill was 14.8sec ahead of Villeneuve and coming up to lap Ricardo Rosset's Footwork which was battling hard for 16th place with the Tyrrell of Ukyo Katayama. The two men were paying scant attention to their rear-view mirrors as they concentrated on their own personal dispute. Hill simply could not get by.

Between laps 21 and 23, Hill dropped from 14.8 to 7.1sec ahead of Villeneuve, losing 5.8sec on lap 22 alone as he struggled to get past the slower cars. On lap 23 he had successfully lapped Rosset, but was still lapping 2sec slower than Villeneuve as he struggled to overtake Katayama, a task which occupied him until the end of lap 24.

With a clear track ahead of him again, the race leader managed to stabilise his advantage, even opening it out to 9.8sec by the end of lap 29. But by the time the two Williams drivers emerged from their second refuelling stops, on laps 30 and 31 respectively, Villeneuve had scented a possible victory. By lap 37 he was only 2.5sec behind Hill. On lap 39 the gap was just 0.802 sec.

The situation now developed into a stalemate. Villeneuve felt he could have lapped faster on a clear track, but Hill was in a position to dictate the pace of the race provided, of course, that he didn't make a slip. It was now clear that the outcome of this potential championship decider was likely to hinge on the speed of their final refuelling stops.

At the end of lap 49, Hill was scheduled to come in. Unfortunately, he found himself following David Coulthard's McLaren, limping in with a punctured rear tyre, at the last right-hander before the pits and had to swoop wide round the outside of his former team-mate before darting back across the track into the pit lane entrance road.

Although he would later suggest this cost him more time, in fact Hill's 'in lap' prior to his third and final refuelling stop was completed in 1m 30.826s. Villeneuve came in next time round in 1m 30.754s. The two Williams FW18s were now less than two seconds apart on the road, but the final blow for Hill came when he was held for a couple of crucial seconds after the completion of his refuelling while Coulthard pulled into the McLaren pits a few yards further on.

Thus, as Hill hurtled past the pits to complete his 50th lap, Villeneuve was accelerating hard down the pit lane to return to the race, just managing to squeeze out and into the first corner before his rival.

It was all too easy to blame Hill's failure to win the race on that slight, final delay in the pit lane, yet such a conclusion presents a dramatically distorted picture of the events which led to his defeat. When Jacques Villeneuve took fourth place from Michael Schumacher in an audacious lunge round the outside of the final right-hander before the pits as the two cars came up to complete lap 16, the real difference between the two Williams drivers was thrown into graphic relief.

Villeneuve took a massive risk because he knew he had nothing to lose. Hill had everything to lose, yet with victory virtually in the palm of his hand, he still couldn't prevent this slipping away.

It was now win or bust for Villeneuve in the Japanese GP at Suzuka, a circuit he knew well after competing in Japanese Formula 3. Hill needed just one point to secure the title. He looked to be well advised to keep out of trouble and cruise round to clinch it with a fourth or fifth place finish. Given his recent luck, racing for another win might be too much of a gamble.

And there were more surprises to come. On the Friday after finishing second at Estoril, Hill had his own stunning announcement to make – that he had signed a one-year contract to join Tom Walkinshaw's TWR Arrows team for 1997.

As the *Daily Telegraph* succinctly pointed out, this was F1's equivalent to Alan Shearer signing for Rochdale. Yet maybe not. With the support of the Bridgestone tyre company, and with a Yamaha works engine deal in the pipeline, confirmed in the week prior to the Japanese Grand Prix, Hill reckoned he was going to be in on the ground floor of something big.

No hard feelings. Damon exchanges a word with Heinz-Harald Frentzen, the man Frank Williams signed to replace him for 1997 (ICN UK Bureau).

Walkinshaw is a relentlessly determined Scot, used to succeeding. His international design, engineering and manufacturing group boasts a blue chip clientele, a £250 million turnover and a workforce of 1,200. His racing team has won in every category in which it has competed, most notably Le Mans in 1988 and 1990, and the World Sports Car Championship in 1987, 1988 and 1991.

As engineering director at Benetton, Walkinshaw played a major part in Schumacher's World Championship successes. A formidable team builder, he now had serious ambitions for his own new Arrows equipe and was looking for a top driver to lead the recovery. For Hill, offered a tempting financial and technical deal, this seemed a gamble worth taking.

Meanwhile it now remained to be seen whether the title leader could finish the job at Suzuka. On Sunday, 13 October 1996, he and his new Scottish boss would discover if the TWR Arrows team would carry the World Champion's coveted race Number 1 into the 1997 season.

As he sprayed the champagne with Walkinshaw, both men all smiles, on the steps of the Conrad Hotel, Damon Hill was just over two weeks away from his first World Championship. For all his outward bullishness, at 36 years of age he must have realised that here was his final shot. No more chances if he missed the target this time.

Could he do it? That final fortnight to Suzuka would seem like an eternity.

Damon Hill's career statistics

NC = Non-Championship; DIS = disqualified; DNF = did not finish; DNS = did not start; P = pole; FL = fastest lap; R = retired.

THE MOTORCYCLE YEARS
1984

Champion of Brands, riding a Yamaha TZ 350 with over 40 wins.

THE CAR YEARS
1984

First car win, driving a Formula Ford 1600 machine at Brands Hatch. Received special commendation in the end-of-season Grovewood Awards after only half a season racing.

1985

Contested a full programme of FF1600 in Van Diemen fielded by Manadient Racing, third in Esso FF1600 championship and fifth in the Townsend Thoresen FF1600 championship with six race wins. Finished third in Formula Ford Festival at Brands Hatch and earned third prize in the Grovewood Awards.

1986

British Formula 3 championship

9 Mar	Thruxton	Ralt RT30/86 VW	DNF
23 Mar	Silverstone	Ralt RT30/86 VW	10th
31 Mar	Thruxton	Ralt RT30/86 VW	DNF

13 Apr	Silverstone	Ralt RT30/86 VW	DNF
20 Apr	Brands Hatch	Ralt RT30/86 VW	DNF
5 May	Thruxton	Ralt RT30/86 VW	8th
18 May	Donington Park	Ralt RT30/86 VW	5th
25 May	Silverstone	Ralt RT30/86 VW	6th
8 June	Silverstone GP	Ralt RT30/86 VW	9th
21 June	Oulton Park	Ralt RT30/86 VW	4th
29 June	Zandvoort	Ralt RT30/86 VW	5th
13 July	Brands Hatch	Ralt RT30/86 VW	DNF
20 July	Donington Park	Ralt RT30/86 VW	DNF
3 Aug	Brands Hatch	Ralt RT30/86 VW	DNF
10 Aug	Snetterton	Ralt RT30/86 VW	2nd
25 Aug	Silverstone	Ralt RT30/86 VW	DNF
31 Aug	Brands Hatch	Ralt RT30/86 VW	6th
13 Sept	Spa	Ralt RT30/86 VW	DNF
28 Sept	Zolder	Ralt RT30/86 VW	DNF
5 Oct	Silverstone GP	Ralt RT30/86 VW	DNF
23 Nov	Macau	Ralt RT30/86 VW	DNF

British F3 championship: 9th equal with Keith Fine.

1987

British Formula 3 championship

15 Mar	Thruxton	Ralt RT31 Toyota	DNF
5 Apr	Brands Hatch	Ralt RT31 Toyota	3rd
12 Apr	Silverstone GP	Ralt RT31 Toyota	DNF
20 Apr	Thruxton	Ralt RT31 Toyota	DNF
4 May	Silverstone	Ralt RT31 Toyota	5th
17 May	Brands Hatch	Ralt RT31 Toyota	7th
25 May	Thruxton	Ralt RT31 Toyota	5th
7 June	Silverstone	Ralt RT31 Toyota	4th
28 June	Zandvoort	Ralt RT31 Toyota	1st/FL
5 July	Donington Park	Ralt RT31 Toyota	DNF
12 July	Silverstone GP	Ralt RT31 Toyota	5th
2 Aug	Snetterton	Ralt RT31 Toyota	DNF
9 Aug	Donington Park	Ralt RT31 Toyota	DNF
15 Aug	Oulton Park	Ralt RT31 Toyota	3rd
31 Aug	Silverstone	Ralt RT31 Toyota	2nd
6 Sept	Brands Hatch	Ralt RT31 Toyota	2nd
13 Sept	Spa	Ralt RT31 Toyota	1st/FL
11 Oct	Brands Hatch	Ralt RT31 Toyota	10th
18 Oct	Thruxton	Ralt RT31 Toyota	DNF
29 Nov	Macau	Ralt RT31 Toyota	DNF

British F3 championship: 5th overall.

1988

British F3 championship

13 Mar	Thruxton	Ralt RT32 Toyota	3rd
27 Mar	Silverstone	Ralt RT32 Toyota	6th
4 Apr	Thruxton	Ralt RT32 Toyota	DNF/FL
17 Apr	Brands Hatch	Ralt RT32 Toyota	2nd
24 Apr	Donington Park	Ralt RT32 Toyota	4th
2 May	Silverstone	Ralt RT32 Toyota	3rd
14 May	Monaco F3 GP	Ralt RT32 Toyota	6th
22 May	Brands Hatch	Ralt RT32 Toyota	DNF
30 May	Thruxton	Ralt RT32 Toyota	1st
5 June	Silverstone GP	Ralt RT32 Toyota	DNF
3 July	Donington Park	Ralt RT32 Toyota	4th
9 July	Silverstone GP	Ralt RT32 Toyota	1st
31 July	Snetterton	Ralt RT32 Toyota	DNF
21 Aug	Oulton Park	Ralt RT32 Toyota	3rd
29 Aug	Silverstone	Ralt RT32 Toyota	DNF
4 Sept	Brands Hatch	Ralt RT32 Toyota	2nd
17 Sept	Spa	Ralt RT32 Toyota	4th
25 Sept	Thruxton	Ralt RT32 Toyota	3rd
2 Oct	Silverstone GP	Ralt RT32 Toyota	10th
9 Oct	Brands Hatch NC	Ralt RT32 Toyota	DNF
16 Oct	Zolder	F3000 Lola T88/50	DNF
23 Oct	Dijon-Prenois	F3000 Lola T88/50	8th
27 Nov	Macau	Ralt RT32 Toyota	2nd

British F3 championship: 3rd overall.

1989

15 Apr	Oulton Park	F3000 Reynard 88D	3rd
10/11 June	Le Mans	Porsche 962GTi	DNF
	(sharing with Steven Anskar and David Hobbs)		
23 July	*Enna Pergusa	Footwork MC041	DNF
20 Aug	*Brands Hatch	Footwork MC041	DNF
28 Aug	*Birmingham	Footwork MC041	DNS
16 Sept	*Spa	Footwork MC041	14th
24 Sept	*Le Mans	Footwork MC041	16th
22 Oct	*Dijon-Prenois	Footwork MC041	15th

* FIA International F3000 championship rounds; no points scored.

1990

FIA International F3000 championship

22 Apr	Donington Park	Lola T90/50	DNS

19 May	Silverstone	Lola T90/50	DNF
4 June	Pau	Lola T90/50	DNF
17 June	Jerez	Lola T90/50	7th
24 June	Monza	Lola T90/50	11th
22 July	Enna Pergusa	Lola T90/50	9th/FL
28 July	Hockenheim	Lola T90/50	DNF
19 Aug	Brands Hatch	Lola T90/50	2nd
27 Aug	Birmingham	Lola T90/50	DNF
23 Sept	Le Mans	Lola T90/50	DNF
7 Oct	Nogaro	Lola T90/50	10th

F3000 championship: 13th equal with Antonio Tamburini.

1991

FIA International F3000 championship

14 Apr	Vallelunga	Lola T91/50	4th
20 May	Pau	Lola T91/50	DNF
9 June	Jerez	Lola T91/50	8th
23 June	Mugello	Lola T91/50	DNF
7 July	Enna Pergusa	Lola T91/50	11th
27 July	Hockenheim	Lola T91/50	DNF
18 Aug	Brands Hatch	Lola T91/50	6th
24 Aug	Spa	Lola T91/40	DNF
22 Sept	Le Mans	Lola T91/50	4th
6 Oct	Nogaro	Reynard 91D	3rd

F3000 championship: 7th overall.

1992

Formula 1

3 May	Spanish GP Barcelona	Brabham BT60B	DNQ
17 May	San Marino GP Imola	Brabham BT60B	DNQ
31 May	Monaco GP M'Carlo	Brabham BT60B	DNQ
14 June	Canadian GP Montreal	Brabham BT60B	DNQ
5 July	French GP Magny-Cours	Brabham BT60B	DNQ
12 July	British GP Silverstone	Brabham BT60B	16th
26 July	German GP Hockenheim	Brabham BT60B	DNQ
16 Aug	Hungarian GP Hungaroring	Brabham BT60B	11th

No championship points scored.

1993

14 Mar	South African GP Kyalami	Williams FW15C	DNF
28 Mar	Brazilian GP Interlagos	Williams FW15C	2nd
11 Apr	European GP Donington	Williams FW15C	2nd

25 Apr	San Marino GP Imola	Williams FW15C	DNF
9 May	Spanish GP Barcelona	Williams FW15C	DNF
23 May	Monaco GP M'Carlo	Williams FW15C	2nd
13 June	Canadian GP Montreal	Williams FW15C	3rd
4 July	French GP Magny-Cours	Williams FW15C	2nd/P
11 July	British GP Silverstone	Williams FW15C	DNF
25 July	German GP Hockenheim	Williams FW15C	15th
15 Aug	Hungarian GP Hungaroring	Williams FW15C	1st
29 Aug	Belgian GP Spa	Williams FW15C	1st
12 Sept	Italian GP Monza	Williams FW15C	1st/FL
26 Sept	Portuguese GP Estoril	Williams FW15C	3rd/P/FL
24 Oct	Japanese GP Suzuka	Williams FW15C	4th
7 Nov	Australian GP Adelaide	Williams FW15C	3rd

World Championship placing: 3rd, 69 points.
Alain Prost (World Champion) scored 99 points.

1994

27 Mar	Brazilian GP Interlagos	Williams FW16	2nd
17 Apr	Pacific GP TIA Aida	Williams FW16	DNF
1 May	San Marino GP Imola	Williams FW16	6th/FL
15 May	Monaco GP M'Carlo	Williams FW16	DNF
29 May	Spanish GP Barcelona	Williams FW16	1st
12 June	Canadian GP Montreal	Williams FW16	2nd
3 July	French GP Magny-Cours	Williams FW16	2nd/P/FL
10 July	British GP Silverstone	Williams FW16	1st/P/FL
31 July	German GP Hockenheim	Williams FW16	8th
14 Aug	Hungarian GP Hungaroring	Williams FW16	2nd
28 Aug	Belgian GP Spa	Williams FW16	1st/FL
11 Sept	Italian GP Monza	Williams FW16	1st/FL
25 Sept	Portuguese GP Estoril	Williams FW16	1st
16 Oct	European GP Jerez	Williams FW16	2nd
6 Nov	Japanese GP Suzuka	Williams FW16	1st/FL
13 Nov	Australian GP Adelaide	Williams FW16	DNF

World Championship placing: 2nd, 91 points.
World Champion Michael Schumacher scored 92 points.

1995

24 Mar	Brazilian GP Interlagos	Williams FW17	DNF/P
9 Apr	Argentine GP B'Aires	Williams FW17	1st
30 Apr	San Marino GP Imola	Williams FW17	1st
14 May	Spanish GP Barcelona	Williams FW17	4th/FL
28 May	Monaco GP M'Carlo	Williams FW17	2nd/P
11 June	Canadian GP Montreal	Williams FW17	DNF

2 July	French GP Magny-Cours	Williams FW17	2nd/P
16 July	British GP Silverstone	Williams FW17	DNF/P/FL
30 July	German GP Hockenheim	Williams FW17	DNF/P
13 Aug	Hungarian GP Hungaroring	Williams FW17	1st/P/FL
27 Aug	Belgian GP Spa	Williams FW17	2nd
10 Sept	Italian GP Monza	Williams FW17	DNF
24 Sept	Portuguese GP Estoril	Williams FW17B	3rd
1 Oct	European GP Nurburgring	Williams FW17B	DNF
22 Oct	Pacific GP TI Aida	Williams FW17B	3rd
29 Oct	Japanese GP Suzuka	Williams FW17B	DNF
12 Nov	Australian GP Adelaide	Williams FW17B	1st/P/FL

World Championship placing: 2nd, 69 points.
World Champion Michael Schumacher scored 102 point.

1996

10 Mar	Australian GP Melbourne	Williams FW18	1st
31 Mar	Brazilian GP Interlagos	Williams FW18	1st/P/FL
7 Apr	Argentine GP B'Aires	Williams FW18	1st/P
28 Apr	European GP Nurburgring	Williams FW18	4th/P/FL
5 May	San Marino GP Imola	Williams FW18	1st/FL
19 May	Monaco GP M'Carlo	Williams FW18	DNF
2 June	Spanish GP Barcelona	Williams FW18	DNF/P
16 June	Canadian GP Montreal	Williams FW18	1st/P
30 June	French GP Magny-Cours	Williams FW18	1st
14 July	British GP Silverstone	Williams FW18	DNF/P
28 July	German GP Hockenheim	Williams FW18	1st/P
11 Aug	Hungarian GP, Hungaroring	Williams FW18	2nd/FL
25 Aug	Belgian GP, Spa	Williams FW18	5th
8 Sept	Italian GP, Monza	Williams FW18	DNF/P
22 Sept	Portuguese GP, Estoril	Williams FW18	2nd/P
13 Oct	Japanese GP, Suzuka	Williams FW18	1st

World Championship placing: 1st, 97 points.
Second, Jacques Villeneuve, 78 points; third, Michael Schumacher, 59 points.

Index

Other motorsport biographies of interest
from Haynes Publishing:

EDDIE IRVINE
by Adam Cooper

JOHNNY HERBERT
The steel behind the smile
by Christopher Hilton

JACQUES VILLENEUVE
In his own right
by Christopher Hilton

JEAN ALESI
Against the odds
by Christopher Hilton

DAVID COULTHARD
The Flying Scotsman
by Jim Dunn

NIGEL MANSELL
The lion at bay
by Christopher Hilton

MICHAEL SCHUMACHER
Defending the crown
by Christopher Hilton

AYRTON SENNA
The legend grows
by Christopher Hilton

DAMON HILL
From zero to hero
by Alan Henry

JAMES HUNT
Portrait of a champion
by Christopher Hilton